50 St. Patrick's Day Dinner Recipes for Home

By: Kelly Johnson

Table of Contents

- Corned Beef and Cabbage
- Irish Stew
- Shepherd's Pie
- Beef and Guinness Pie
- Bangers and Mash
- Irish Soda Bread
- Colcannon
- Dublin Coddle
- Lamb Stew
- Fish and Chips
- Irish Boxty (Potato Pancakes)
- Irish Beef and Vegetable Soup
- Soda Bread Pizza
- Pork and Apple Stew
- Beef and Root Vegetable Hash
- Irish Salmon with Mustard Glaze
- Chicken and Leek Pie
- Irish Breakfast Casserole
- Grilled Corned Beef Sandwiches
- Guinness BBQ Ribs
- Potato and Onion Gratin
- Irish Stuffed Cabbage Rolls
- Traditional Irish Roast Beef
- Irish-Style Pork Chops
- Lamb and Barley Soup
- Creamy Irish Potato Soup
- Irish Cheddar Mac and Cheese
- Potato and Leek Soup
- Braised Beef with Root Vegetables
- Irish Meatballs with Cabbage
- Corned Beef Hash
- Shepherd's Pie with Sweet Potato Topping
- Guinness Braised Short Ribs
- Irish Chicken Stew
- Irish Seafood Chowder
- Stuffed Shepherd's Pie

- Irish Brown Bread
- Irish Herb Roasted Chicken
- Beef and Ale Pie
- Irish Caramelized Onion Soup
- Dublin Bay Prawns with Garlic Butter
- Corned Beef Tacos
- Irish Lamb Chops with Mint Jelly
- Cottage Pie with Vegetables
- Irish Cheddar and Chive Biscuits
- Irish Baked Potatoes with Sour Cream
- Guinness Beef Stroganoff
- Traditional Irish Roast Pork
- Irish Green Beans with Bacon
- Spiced Irish Lamb Stew

Corned Beef and Cabbage

Ingredients:

- 3-4 lbs corned beef brisket (with spice packet)
- 1 onion, quartered
- 2-3 cloves garlic, minced
- 4-5 carrots, peeled and cut into chunks
- 4-5 potatoes, peeled and cut into chunks
- 1 small head of cabbage, cut into wedges
- 2 bay leaves
- 1 teaspoon black peppercorns
- 1 teaspoon mustard seeds
- 2-3 cups water or beef broth
- Optional: 1-2 cups beer (such as Guinness) for extra flavor

Instructions:

1. **Prepare the Corned Beef:**
    - Rinse the corned beef under cold water to remove excess salt and brine.
    - Place the corned beef in a large pot or slow cooker.
2. **Add Flavorings:**
    - Add the spice packet that came with the corned beef.
    - Add bay leaves, black peppercorns, and mustard seeds.
3. **Cook the Beef:**
    - Pour in enough water or beef broth to cover the meat.
    - If using, add beer for additional flavor.
    - Bring to a boil, then reduce heat to low and cover.
    - Simmer for about 3-4 hours, or until the meat is tender. If using a slow cooker, cook on low for 8-10 hours.
4. **Add Vegetables:**
    - About 1 hour before the beef is done, add the carrots and potatoes to the pot.
    - Continue to cook until the vegetables and beef are tender.
5. **Prepare the Cabbage:**
    - Remove the corned beef from the pot and place it on a cutting board to rest.
    - Add the cabbage wedges to the pot with vegetables. Cook for 20-30 minutes, or until the cabbage is tender.
6. **Serve:**
    - Slice the corned beef against the grain.
    - Serve the sliced corned beef with the cabbage, carrots, and potatoes on the side.
    - Optionally, drizzle some of the cooking liquid over the meat and vegetables.

Tips:

- For a richer flavor, consider cooking the corned beef with a bit of beer.

- You can also use a pressure cooker to reduce cooking time significantly.

Enjoy your classic St. Patrick's Day meal!

Irish Stew

Ingredients:

- 2 lbs lamb or beef stew meat, cut into chunks
- 1/4 cup all-purpose flour
- 2 tablespoons vegetable oil
- 1 large onion, chopped
- 3 cloves garlic, minced
- 4-5 carrots, peeled and sliced
- 4-5 potatoes, peeled and cut into chunks
- 2-3 parsnips, peeled and sliced (optional)
- 1 cup frozen or fresh peas (optional)
- 4 cups beef or lamb broth
- 1 cup Guinness or other dark beer (optional)
- 2 tablespoons tomato paste
- 2 bay leaves
- 1 teaspoon dried thyme
- Salt and black pepper to taste
- 1 tablespoon chopped fresh parsley (for garnish)

Instructions:

1. **Prepare the Meat:**
    - Toss the meat chunks with flour, salt, and pepper.
    - Heat vegetable oil in a large pot or Dutch oven over medium-high heat.
2. **Brown the Meat:**
    - Add the meat to the pot in batches, if necessary, to avoid overcrowding.
    - Brown the meat on all sides, then remove it from the pot and set aside.
3. **Cook the Aromatics:**
    - In the same pot, add chopped onion and cook until softened, about 5 minutes.
    - Add minced garlic and cook for another 1 minute, until fragrant.
4. **Add Liquids and Seasonings:**
    - Stir in tomato paste and cook for 1-2 minutes.
    - Return the browned meat to the pot.
    - Pour in the broth and beer (if using), and bring to a simmer.
    - Add bay leaves, thyme, and additional salt and pepper to taste.
5. **Simmer the Stew:**
    - Reduce the heat to low, cover the pot, and let it simmer for 1.5 to 2 hours, or until the meat is tender.
6. **Add Vegetables:**
    - Add carrots, potatoes, and parsnips (if using) to the pot.
    - Continue to simmer for another 30-40 minutes, or until the vegetables are tender.
7. **Finish and Serve:**
    - If using peas, stir them in during the last 5 minutes of cooking.

- Remove bay leaves and adjust seasoning if needed.
- Garnish with chopped fresh parsley before serving.

Tips:

- For a richer flavor, use a mix of beef and lamb, or stick with one of them based on your preference.
- Serve with crusty Irish soda bread or a simple green salad.

Enjoy your hearty and comforting Irish stew!

Shepherd's Pie

Ingredients:

For the Meat Filling:

- 1 lb ground lamb (or beef for Cottage Pie)
- 1 medium onion, finely chopped
- 2 cloves garlic, minced
- 2 carrots, peeled and diced
- 1 cup frozen peas
- 1 cup beef or lamb broth
- 1 tablespoon tomato paste
- 1 tablespoon Worcestershire sauce
- 1 teaspoon dried thyme
- 1 teaspoon dried rosemary
- Salt and black pepper to taste
- 2 tablespoons all-purpose flour (optional, for thickening)

For the Mashed Potatoes:

- 2 lbs potatoes, peeled and cut into chunks
- 1/4 cup milk
- 3 tablespoons butter
- Salt and black pepper to taste
- 1/4 cup shredded cheddar cheese (optional, for a cheesy topping)

Instructions:

1. **Prepare the Potatoes:**
   - Place the peeled and cut potatoes in a large pot and cover with cold water.
   - Bring to a boil, then reduce heat and simmer until the potatoes are tender, about 15-20 minutes.
   - Drain the potatoes and return them to the pot.
2. **Mash the Potatoes:**
   - Add butter and milk to the potatoes.
   - Mash until smooth and creamy.
   - Season with salt and black pepper to taste.
   - If desired, stir in shredded cheddar cheese.
3. **Prepare the Meat Filling:**
   - While the potatoes are cooking, heat a large skillet over medium heat.
   - Add the ground lamb and cook until browned, breaking it up with a spoon as it cooks.
   - Remove the cooked meat and set aside. Drain excess fat from the skillet.
4. **Cook the Vegetables:**

- In the same skillet, add the chopped onion and cook until softened, about 5 minutes.
- Add minced garlic and cook for an additional minute.
- Stir in the diced carrots and cook for 5 minutes until they start to soften.

5. **Combine Ingredients:**
    - Return the browned meat to the skillet.
    - Stir in the tomato paste and cook for 1-2 minutes.
    - Add Worcestershire sauce, thyme, rosemary, and broth. Bring to a simmer.
    - If the mixture is too watery, you can mix flour with a little water and stir it into the filling to thicken.
    - Add frozen peas and cook for another 5 minutes.
    - Season with salt and black pepper to taste.

6. **Assemble the Pie:**
    - Preheat your oven to 400°F (200°C).
    - Transfer the meat filling into a baking dish.
    - Spread the mashed potatoes evenly over the meat filling.
    - Use a fork to create a pattern on the mashed potatoes if desired, which will help them crisp up in the oven.

7. **Bake:**
    - Bake in the preheated oven for 20-25 minutes, or until the top is golden and the filling is bubbling.
    - If you want a crispier top, place under the broiler for an additional 2-3 minutes, watching closely to avoid burning.

8. **Serve:**
    - Let the Shepherd's Pie rest for a few minutes before serving.

Tips:

- Shepherd's Pie can be made ahead of time and stored in the refrigerator for up to 2 days, or frozen for up to 3 months.
- To freeze, assemble the pie but do not bake. Wrap tightly and freeze. To cook, thaw overnight in the refrigerator and bake as directed.

Enjoy this hearty and comforting dish!

Beef and Guinness Pie

Ingredients:

For the Filling:

- 2 lbs beef chuck or stew meat, cut into bite-sized pieces
- 1/4 cup all-purpose flour
- 2 tablespoons vegetable oil
- 1 large onion, chopped
- 2 cloves garlic, minced
- 3 carrots, peeled and diced
- 2 celery stalks, diced
- 1 tablespoon tomato paste
- 1 cup Guinness beer (or another stout)
- 2 cups beef broth
- 1 tablespoon Worcestershire sauce
- 1 teaspoon dried thyme
- 1 teaspoon dried rosemary
- 1 bay leaf
- Salt and black pepper to taste
- 1 cup frozen peas (optional)
- 1 tablespoon cornstarch mixed with 2 tablespoons water (for thickening, optional)

For the Pie Crust:

- 2 1/2 cups all-purpose flour
- 1 teaspoon salt
- 1 cup (2 sticks) unsalted butter, cold and cut into cubes
- 6-8 tablespoons ice water
- 1 egg, beaten (for egg wash)

Instructions:

1. **Prepare the Beef:**
   - Toss the beef chunks with flour, salt, and pepper.
   - Heat vegetable oil in a large pot or Dutch oven over medium-high heat.
   - Add the beef in batches, if necessary, to avoid overcrowding. Brown on all sides. Remove and set aside.
2. **Cook the Vegetables:**
   - In the same pot, add chopped onion, carrots, and celery. Cook until softened, about 5-7 minutes.
   - Add minced garlic and cook for another minute.
3. **Make the Sauce:**
   - Stir in the tomato paste and cook for 1-2 minutes.

- Return the browned beef to the pot.
- Pour in the Guinness beer and beef broth. Stir to combine.
- Add Worcestershire sauce, thyme, rosemary, and bay leaf.
- Bring to a simmer, then reduce heat to low. Cover and cook for 1.5 to 2 hours, or until the beef is tender.

4. **Thicken the Filling:**
   - If you prefer a thicker filling, stir in the cornstarch mixture and cook for another 5 minutes, until thickened.
   - If using, add frozen peas and cook for 5 minutes more.
   - Remove the bay leaf and adjust seasoning with salt and pepper to taste.

5. **Prepare the Pie Crust:**
   - In a large bowl, whisk together flour and salt.
   - Cut in the cold butter using a pastry cutter or your fingers until the mixture resembles coarse crumbs.
   - Gradually add ice water, 1 tablespoon at a time, until the dough comes together.
   - Divide the dough into two discs, wrap in plastic wrap, and chill in the refrigerator for at least 30 minutes.

6. **Assemble the Pie:**
   - Preheat your oven to 400°F (200°C).
   - Roll out one disc of dough on a lightly floured surface to fit your pie dish.
   - Transfer the dough to the pie dish and press it into the bottom and sides.
   - Fill with the beef mixture.
   - Roll out the second disc of dough and place it over the filling. Trim and crimp the edges to seal.
   - Cut a few slits in the top crust to allow steam to escape.
   - Brush the top with beaten egg for a golden finish.

7. **Bake:**
   - Bake in the preheated oven for 30-35 minutes, or until the crust is golden brown and the filling is bubbling.

8. **Serve:**
   - Allow the pie to cool for a few minutes before serving.

Tips:

- You can prepare the filling ahead of time and store it in the refrigerator for up to 2 days before assembling the pie.
- For an extra touch, sprinkle some freshly chopped parsley over the pie before serving.

Enjoy this rich and comforting Beef and Guinness Pie!

Bangers and Mash

Ingredients:

For the Sausages (Bangers):

- 8 pork sausages (or your preferred type of sausages)
- 1 tablespoon vegetable oil

For the Mashed Potatoes:

- 2 lbs potatoes (Yukon Gold or Russet), peeled and cut into chunks
- 1/4 cup milk
- 3 tablespoons butter
- Salt and black pepper to taste

For the Onion Gravy:

- 2 tablespoons vegetable oil
- 2 large onions, thinly sliced
- 2 cloves garlic, minced
- 2 tablespoons all-purpose flour
- 1 cup beef or chicken broth
- 1 tablespoon Worcestershire sauce
- 1 teaspoon dried thyme
- Salt and black pepper to taste

Instructions:

1. **Cook the Sausages:**
   - Heat vegetable oil in a large skillet over medium heat.
   - Add the sausages and cook, turning occasionally, until browned and cooked through, about 12-15 minutes.
   - Remove sausages from the skillet and set aside.
2. **Prepare the Mashed Potatoes:**
   - Place the potatoes in a large pot and cover with cold water.
   - Bring to a boil, then reduce heat and simmer until potatoes are tender, about 15-20 minutes.
   - Drain the potatoes and return them to the pot.
   - Add butter and milk, and mash until smooth and creamy.
   - Season with salt and black pepper to taste.
3. **Make the Onion Gravy:**
   - In the same skillet used for the sausages, add vegetable oil over medium heat.
   - Add sliced onions and cook, stirring frequently, until caramelized and golden brown, about 10 minutes.
   - Add minced garlic and cook for an additional 1 minute.

        - Stir in flour and cook for 1-2 minutes to form a roux.
        - Gradually add broth, stirring constantly to avoid lumps.
        - Stir in Worcestershire sauce and dried thyme.
        - Bring to a simmer and cook until thickened, about 5 minutes.
        - Season with salt and black pepper to taste.
    4. **Serve:**
        - Return the sausages to the skillet with the gravy and heat through.
        - Spoon mashed potatoes onto plates and top with sausages and onion gravy.

Tips:

- For extra flavor, consider adding a splash of red wine or a bit of mustard to the gravy.
- You can make the onion gravy ahead of time and reheat it when ready to serve.

Enjoy this hearty and comforting British classic!

Irish Soda Bread

Ingredients:

- 4 cups all-purpose flour
- 1 teaspoon baking soda
- 1/2 teaspoon salt
- 1 3/4 cups buttermilk (or milk with 1 tablespoon lemon juice or white vinegar)
- 2 tablespoons sugar (optional, for a slightly sweet bread)
- 1/2 cup raisins or currants (optional)

Instructions:

1. **Preheat Oven:**
   - Preheat your oven to 425°F (220°C). Grease a 9-inch round cake pan or line a baking sheet with parchment paper.
2. **Mix Dry Ingredients:**
   - In a large bowl, whisk together the flour, baking soda, salt, and sugar (if using).
3. **Add Raisins/Currants:**
   - If using, stir in the raisins or currants to coat them lightly with flour.
4. **Add Buttermilk:**
   - Make a well in the center of the dry ingredients.
   - Pour the buttermilk into the well.
   - Gently stir with a wooden spoon or your hands until the dough just comes together. Do not overmix.
5. **Shape the Dough:**
   - Turn the dough out onto a floured surface and knead it lightly just until it forms a rough ball. Be careful not to overwork the dough.
   - Shape the dough into a round loaf and place it on the prepared pan or baking sheet.
   - Use a sharp knife to cut a deep cross into the top of the dough. This helps the bread cook evenly and gives it a traditional look.
6. **Bake:**
   - Bake in the preheated oven for 35-45 minutes, or until the bread is golden brown and sounds hollow when tapped on the bottom.
   - The internal temperature should be around 190°F (88°C).
7. **Cool:**
   - Let the bread cool on a wire rack before slicing.

Tips:

- If you don't have buttermilk, you can use regular milk with 1 tablespoon of lemon juice or white vinegar. Let it sit for 5-10 minutes before using.
- For a slightly crustier bread, place an oven-safe dish of water on the lower rack while baking to create steam.

Enjoy your homemade Irish soda bread with butter, jam, or as an accompaniment to your favorite dishes!

Colcannon

Ingredients:

- 2 lbs potatoes (Yukon Gold or Russet), peeled and cut into chunks
- 4 tablespoons butter, divided
- 1/2 cup milk or cream
- 1 small head of cabbage, chopped (about 4 cups)
- 4 green onions, chopped
- Salt and black pepper to taste

Instructions:

1. **Cook the Potatoes:**
    - Place the peeled and cut potatoes in a large pot and cover with cold water.
    - Bring to a boil over medium-high heat, then reduce the heat and simmer until the potatoes are tender, about 15-20 minutes.
    - Drain the potatoes well.
2. **Mash the Potatoes:**
    - Return the drained potatoes to the pot.
    - Add 2 tablespoons of butter and milk (or cream). Mash until smooth and creamy.
    - Season with salt and black pepper to taste. Set aside.
3. **Prepare the Cabbage:**
    - While the potatoes are cooking, melt the remaining 2 tablespoons of butter in a large skillet over medium heat.
    - Add the chopped cabbage and cook, stirring occasionally, until it is tender and slightly caramelized, about 10-15 minutes.
    - Stir in the chopped green onions and cook for an additional 2-3 minutes.
4. **Combine:**
    - Gently fold the cooked cabbage and green onions into the mashed potatoes until well combined.
5. **Serve:**
    - Transfer the Colcannon to a serving dish and make a small well in the center.
    - Place a pat of butter in the well and let it melt into the Colcannon.
    - Garnish with additional chopped green onions if desired.

Tips:

- Colcannon is often served with additional melted butter on top, but you can also use a dollop of sour cream or plain yogurt for extra richness.
- For added flavor, you can mix in some cooked bacon or ham.

Enjoy this comforting and traditional Irish side dish!

Dublin Coddle

Ingredients:

- 1 lb pork sausages (preferably Irish bangers, but any good quality sausage will work)
- 1 lb pork shoulder or bacon, cut into chunks
- 1 large onion, thinly sliced
- 4 cloves garlic, minced
- 4-5 large potatoes, peeled and sliced into rounds
- 2-3 carrots, peeled and sliced
- 2 cups chicken or beef broth
- 1 cup water (or additional broth)
- 2 tablespoons chopped fresh parsley (or 1 tablespoon dried parsley)
- 1 teaspoon dried thyme
- 1 bay leaf
- Salt and black pepper to taste
- 2 tablespoons vegetable oil (if needed)

Instructions:

1. **Brown the Sausages and Pork:**
    - Preheat your oven to 325°F (165°C).
    - In a large skillet or Dutch oven, heat vegetable oil over medium heat.
    - Add the sausages and brown them on all sides. Remove and set aside.
    - In the same skillet, add the pork shoulder or bacon and brown on all sides. Remove and set aside.
2. **Cook the Vegetables:**
    - In the same pot, add sliced onions and cook until softened, about 5 minutes.
    - Add minced garlic and cook for another 1 minute.
3. **Layer the Coddle:**
    - In a large Dutch oven or oven-proof casserole dish, layer half of the sliced potatoes on the bottom.
    - Add half of the carrots on top of the potatoes.
    - Place the browned sausages and pork chunks on top of the vegetables.
    - Add the remaining potatoes and carrots on top of the meat.
4. **Add Broth and Seasonings:**
    - Pour the chicken or beef broth and water over the layered ingredients.
    - Add the bay leaf, thyme, and parsley. Season with salt and black pepper to taste.
5. **Bake:**
    - Cover the pot with a lid or aluminum foil.
    - Bake in the preheated oven for 2 to 2.5 hours, or until the vegetables are tender and the flavors are well combined.
6. **Finish and Serve:**
    - Remove the bay leaf before serving.
    - Garnish with additional chopped parsley if desired.

Tips:

- For extra flavor, consider adding a splash of Guinness or another stout to the broth.
- Dublin Coddle can be made a day ahead and reheated, as the flavors continue to develop.

Enjoy this classic Irish comfort food, perfect for a hearty meal!

Lamb Stew

Ingredients:

- 2 lbs lamb shoulder or stew meat, cut into bite-sized chunks
- 3 tablespoons vegetable oil
- 1 large onion, chopped
- 3 cloves garlic, minced
- 4 carrots, peeled and sliced
- 3-4 potatoes, peeled and cut into chunks
- 1 cup celery, chopped
- 1 cup frozen or fresh peas
- 1 cup red wine (optional, for richer flavor)
- 2 cups beef or lamb broth
- 1 tablespoon tomato paste
- 2 tablespoons Worcestershire sauce
- 2 bay leaves
- 1 teaspoon dried thyme
- 1 teaspoon dried rosemary
- Salt and black pepper to taste
- 2 tablespoons all-purpose flour (optional, for thickening)
- 1 tablespoon chopped fresh parsley (for garnish)

Instructions:

1. **Brown the Lamb:**
   - Heat vegetable oil in a large pot or Dutch oven over medium-high heat.
   - Add the lamb chunks in batches to avoid overcrowding. Brown the meat on all sides. Remove the meat from the pot and set aside.
2. **Cook the Vegetables:**
   - In the same pot, add a little more oil if needed.
   - Add chopped onion and cook until softened, about 5 minutes.
   - Add minced garlic and cook for another minute.
3. **Build the Stew:**
   - Stir in the tomato paste and cook for 1-2 minutes.
   - Return the browned lamb to the pot.
   - Add the red wine (if using) and cook for a few minutes to let the alcohol evaporate.
   - Pour in the beef or lamb broth and stir in Worcestershire sauce, bay leaves, thyme, and rosemary.
   - Bring to a boil, then reduce heat to low and simmer for 1 hour, covered.
4. **Add Vegetables:**
   - After 1 hour, add the carrots, potatoes, and celery.
   - Continue to simmer for another 30-40 minutes, or until the lamb is tender and the vegetables are cooked.

5. **Thicken the Stew (optional):**
    - If you prefer a thicker stew, mix 2 tablespoons of flour with a little water to form a slurry. Stir the slurry into the stew and cook for an additional 5-10 minutes, until thickened.
6. **Finish and Serve:**
    - Stir in the peas and cook for an additional 5 minutes.
    - Remove bay leaves.
    - Adjust seasoning with salt and black pepper to taste.
    - Garnish with chopped fresh parsley before serving.

Tips:

- For a deeper flavor, you can brown the lamb and vegetables ahead of time and let the stew rest overnight in the refrigerator. Reheat before serving.
- Serve with crusty bread or over mashed potatoes for a complete meal.

Enjoy this warm and comforting lamb stew, perfect for a hearty dinner!

Fish and Chips

Ingredients:

For the Fish:

- 4 large white fish fillets (such as cod, haddock, or pollock), skinless and boneless
- 1 cup all-purpose flour (for dredging)
- 1 cup all-purpose flour (for batter)
- 1 teaspoon baking powder
- 1/2 teaspoon salt
- 1/2 teaspoon black pepper
- 1 cup cold sparkling water or cold beer
- 1 large egg
- Vegetable oil (for frying)

For the Chips:

- 4 large russet potatoes, peeled
- Vegetable oil (for frying)
- Salt (for seasoning)

Instructions:

1. **Prepare the Chips:**
   - Peel and cut the potatoes into thick chips or fries.
   - Rinse the potato slices in cold water to remove excess starch. Pat dry with a kitchen towel.
   - Heat vegetable oil in a large pot or deep fryer to 325°F (165°C).
2. **Cook the Chips:**
   - Fry the potato slices in batches for 3-4 minutes, until they are soft but not yet crispy. Remove with a slotted spoon and drain on paper towels.
   - Increase the oil temperature to 375°F (190°C).
   - Return the chips to the hot oil and fry until golden and crispy, about 3-4 minutes. Remove and drain on paper towels. Season with salt immediately.
3. **Prepare the Fish:**
   - Pat the fish fillets dry with paper towels.
   - Season the fish with salt and pepper.
   - For the batter, in a large bowl, whisk together 1 cup of flour, baking powder, salt, and black pepper.
   - Add the egg and cold sparkling water or beer. Mix until smooth. The batter should be thick enough to coat the fish but still pourable.
4. **Fry the Fish:**
   - Heat vegetable oil in a large pot or deep fryer to 375°F (190°C). Make sure there's enough oil to fully submerge the fish.

- Dredge each fish fillet in the flour (for dredging), then dip into the batter, allowing excess to drip off.
- Carefully lower the battered fish into the hot oil. Fry in batches if necessary to avoid overcrowding.
- Cook for 5-6 minutes, or until the fish is golden brown and crispy, and the fish flakes easily with a fork.
- Remove the fish with a slotted spoon and drain on paper towels.

5. **Serve:**
   - Serve the crispy fish and chips with malt vinegar, tartar sauce, or lemon wedges, and optionally with peas or a side salad.

Tips:

- For extra crispiness, let the battered fish rest for a few minutes before frying.
- You can make a classic mushy peas side dish by cooking and mashing peas with a bit of butter and salt.

Enjoy your classic fish and chips with all the traditional accompaniments!

Irish Boxty (Potato Pancakes)

Ingredients:

- 2 cups raw potatoes, peeled and grated
- 1 cup cooked potatoes, mashed (about 1 large potato)
- 1 small onion, finely chopped (optional)
- 1 cup all-purpose flour
- 1 teaspoon baking powder
- 1/2 teaspoon salt
- 1/4 teaspoon black pepper
- 1/2 cup milk (or more as needed)
- 1 large egg
- 2 tablespoons vegetable oil (for frying)

Instructions:

1. **Prepare the Raw Potatoes:**
   - Peel and grate the raw potatoes. Place the grated potatoes in a clean cloth or paper towel and squeeze out as much moisture as possible.
2. **Prepare the Mashed Potatoes:**
   - Cook and mash the potatoes. Let them cool slightly.
3. **Mix the Ingredients:**
   - In a large bowl, combine the grated raw potatoes, mashed potatoes, and chopped onion (if using).
   - In a separate bowl, whisk together the flour, baking powder, salt, and black pepper.
   - Add the flour mixture to the potato mixture.
   - In a small bowl, whisk the milk and egg together. Add to the potato mixture and mix until just combined. The batter should be thick but pourable. Adjust the milk if needed.
4. **Cook the Boxty:**
   - Heat 1 tablespoon of vegetable oil in a large skillet over medium heat.
   - Drop spoonfuls of the batter into the skillet, flattening each one into a pancake shape with the back of the spoon.
   - Cook for 3-4 minutes on each side, or until golden brown and crispy. Adjust the heat as necessary to avoid burning.
   - Add more oil to the skillet as needed between batches.
5. **Serve:**
   - Serve the boxty hot, with your choice of toppings such as sour cream, applesauce, or a side of bacon or eggs.

Tips:

- For a richer flavor, you can add finely chopped herbs like chives or parsley to the batter.

- Boxty can be served as a side dish or as a main course, depending on your preference.

Enjoy your delicious Irish Boxty!

Irish Beef and Vegetable Soup

Ingredients:

- 1 lb beef stew meat (such as chuck or round), cut into bite-sized pieces
- 2 tablespoons vegetable oil
- 1 large onion, chopped
- 3 cloves garlic, minced
- 3 carrots, peeled and sliced
- 2 celery stalks, chopped
- 4 large potatoes, peeled and diced
- 1 cup green beans or peas (fresh or frozen)
- 6 cups beef broth
- 1 cup water
- 1 tablespoon tomato paste
- 1 teaspoon dried thyme
- 1 teaspoon dried rosemary
- 1 bay leaf
- Salt and black pepper to taste
- 2 tablespoons all-purpose flour (optional, for thickening)
- 1 cup frozen or fresh peas (optional, for added texture)

Instructions:

1. **Brown the Beef:**
    - Heat vegetable oil in a large pot or Dutch oven over medium-high heat.
    - Add the beef stew meat in batches, if necessary, to avoid overcrowding. Brown the meat on all sides. Remove the browned meat and set aside.
2. **Cook the Vegetables:**
    - In the same pot, add a bit more oil if needed.
    - Add chopped onion and cook until softened, about 5 minutes.
    - Add minced garlic and cook for an additional 1 minute.
3. **Build the Soup:**
    - Stir in tomato paste and cook for 1-2 minutes.
    - Return the browned beef to the pot.
    - Add beef broth, water, thyme, rosemary, and bay leaf.
    - Bring to a boil, then reduce heat and let it simmer for 1 hour, or until the beef is tender.
4. **Add Vegetables:**
    - Add carrots, celery, and potatoes to the pot.
    - Continue to simmer for another 20-30 minutes, or until the vegetables are tender.
    - Stir in green beans or peas, and cook for an additional 5 minutes.
5. **Thicken the Soup (optional):**

- If you prefer a thicker soup, mix 2 tablespoons of flour with a little water to form a slurry. Stir the slurry into the soup and cook for an additional 5-10 minutes, until thickened.

6. **Finish and Serve:**
    - Remove the bay leaf.
    - Adjust seasoning with salt and black pepper to taste.
    - Serve hot with crusty bread or rolls.

Tips:

- For extra flavor, you can add a splash of red wine or a bit of Worcestershire sauce to the soup.
- This soup can be made ahead of time and stored in the refrigerator for up to 3 days or frozen for up to 3 months.

Enjoy your hearty and warming Irish Beef and Vegetable Soup!

Soda Bread Pizza

Ingredients:

For the Soda Bread:

- 2 cups all-purpose flour
- 1 teaspoon baking soda
- 1/2 teaspoon salt
- 1 1/2 cups buttermilk (or milk with 1 tablespoon lemon juice or white vinegar)

For the Pizza Topping:

- 1/2 cup tomato sauce (pizza or marinara sauce)
- 1 cup shredded mozzarella cheese
- 1/2 cup grated Parmesan cheese
- 1/2 cup sliced pepperoni or cooked sausage (optional)
- 1/2 cup sliced bell peppers
- 1/2 cup sliced mushrooms
- 1/2 cup sliced black olives
- 1/4 cup thinly sliced red onions
- 1 tablespoon olive oil (for drizzling)
- 1 teaspoon dried oregano or Italian seasoning
- Fresh basil leaves (for garnish, optional)

Instructions:

1. **Prepare the Soda Bread:**
   - Preheat your oven to 425°F (220°C). Line a baking sheet with parchment paper.
   - In a large bowl, whisk together flour, baking soda, and salt.
   - Make a well in the center and pour in the buttermilk. Stir until just combined. The dough will be sticky.
   - Turn the dough onto a lightly floured surface and gently shape it into a rough circle or rectangle, about 1/2 inch thick. Transfer to the prepared baking sheet.
2. **Bake the Soda Bread Crust:**
   - Bake the soda bread crust in the preheated oven for 10-12 minutes, until it's just beginning to set but is not fully cooked. It should be firm to the touch but not browned.
3. **Add Pizza Toppings:**
   - Remove the partially baked soda bread from the oven.
   - Spread tomato sauce evenly over the crust.
   - Sprinkle mozzarella and Parmesan cheeses over the sauce.
   - Add desired toppings (pepperoni, sausage, bell peppers, mushrooms, olives, onions).
   - Drizzle with olive oil and sprinkle with dried oregano or Italian seasoning.

4. **Finish Baking:**
    - Return the pizza to the oven and bake for an additional 10-15 minutes, or until the cheese is melted and bubbly, and the crust is golden brown.
5. **Serve:**
    - Remove from the oven and let cool for a few minutes.
    - Garnish with fresh basil leaves if desired.
    - Slice and serve.

Tips:

- Feel free to customize the toppings based on your preferences or what you have on hand.
- For a crispier crust, you can preheat a pizza stone in the oven and bake the pizza on it.

Enjoy this creative and delicious Soda Bread Pizza!

Pork and Apple Stew

Ingredients:

- 1.5 lbs pork shoulder or pork loin, cut into bite-sized cubes
- 2 tablespoons vegetable oil
- 1 large onion, chopped
- 3 cloves garlic, minced
- 3 large apples, peeled, cored, and chopped (e.g., Granny Smith or another tart variety)
- 4 carrots, peeled and sliced
- 3 celery stalks, chopped
- 4 cups chicken or vegetable broth
- 1 cup dry white wine (optional, or use additional broth)
- 2 tablespoons Dijon mustard
- 1 tablespoon brown sugar
- 1 teaspoon dried thyme
- 1 teaspoon dried rosemary
- 1 bay leaf
- Salt and black pepper to taste
- 2 tablespoons all-purpose flour (optional, for thickening)
- 1 tablespoon chopped fresh parsley (for garnish)

Instructions:

1. **Brown the Pork:**
   - Heat vegetable oil in a large pot or Dutch oven over medium-high heat.
   - Add the pork cubes and brown on all sides. Do this in batches if necessary to avoid overcrowding. Remove the browned pork and set aside.
2. **Cook the Aromatics:**
   - In the same pot, add a bit more oil if needed.
   - Add chopped onion and cook until softened, about 5 minutes.
   - Add minced garlic and cook for an additional minute.
3. **Build the Stew:**
   - Stir in the Dijon mustard, brown sugar, dried thyme, rosemary, and bay leaf.
   - Return the browned pork to the pot.
   - Pour in the chicken or vegetable broth and white wine (if using).
   - Bring to a boil, then reduce the heat and let it simmer for 45 minutes to 1 hour, or until the pork is tender.
4. **Add the Vegetables and Apples:**
   - Add the chopped apples, carrots, and celery to the pot.
   - Continue to simmer for another 20-30 minutes, or until the vegetables are tender and the apples have softened.
5. **Thicken the Stew (optional):**
   - If you prefer a thicker stew, mix 2 tablespoons of flour with a small amount of water to create a slurry.

- Stir the slurry into the stew and cook for an additional 5-10 minutes, until the stew has thickened.
6. **Finish and Serve:**
    - Remove the bay leaf.
    - Adjust seasoning with salt and black pepper to taste.
    - Garnish with chopped fresh parsley before serving.

Tips:

- For extra flavor, consider adding a splash of apple cider vinegar or a few tablespoons of apple cider for a bit more tartness.
- Serve the stew with crusty bread or over mashed potatoes for a complete meal.

Enjoy this hearty and flavorful Pork and Apple Stew!

Beef and Root Vegetable Hash

Ingredients:

- 1 lb cooked beef (such as roast beef or steak), cubed
- 2 tablespoons vegetable oil
- 1 large onion, chopped
- 2 cloves garlic, minced
- 2 carrots, peeled and diced
- 2 parsnips, peeled and diced
- 1 large sweet potato or 2 regular potatoes, peeled and diced
- 1 red bell pepper, diced (optional)
- 1 tablespoon fresh thyme or 1 teaspoon dried thyme
- 1 tablespoon fresh rosemary or 1 teaspoon dried rosemary
- 1 teaspoon paprika
- Salt and black pepper to taste
- 2 tablespoons soy sauce or Worcestershire sauce (optional, for added depth of flavor)
- 2 tablespoons chopped fresh parsley (for garnish)

Instructions:

1. **Prepare the Vegetables:**
   - Heat vegetable oil in a large skillet or sauté pan over medium heat.
   - Add the chopped onion and cook until softened, about 5 minutes.
   - Add minced garlic and cook for another 1 minute.
2. **Cook the Root Vegetables:**
   - Add diced carrots, parsnips, and sweet potatoes (or regular potatoes) to the skillet.
   - Cook, stirring occasionally, until the vegetables start to soften and brown, about 10-15 minutes.
3. **Add the Beef:**
   - Stir in the cubed beef and cook until heated through.
   - Add the diced red bell pepper (if using) and cook for an additional 5 minutes.
4. **Season the Hash:**
   - Stir in fresh or dried thyme, rosemary, paprika, salt, and black pepper.
   - If desired, add soy sauce or Worcestershire sauce for additional flavor. Stir to combine.
5. **Finish Cooking:**
   - Continue to cook the hash until all the vegetables are tender and slightly crispy, about 5-10 more minutes. Adjust seasoning as needed.
6. **Serve:**
   - Garnish with chopped fresh parsley before serving.

Tips:

- Feel free to customize the hash with other vegetables like turnips, rutabagas, or green beans based on what you have on hand.
- For a more savory hash, consider adding a bit of grated cheese on top or a fried egg for a complete meal.

Enjoy your delicious and satisfying Beef and Root Vegetable Hash!

Irish Salmon with Mustard Glaze

Ingredients:

- 4 salmon fillets (about 6 oz each), skinless
- 2 tablespoons olive oil
- 1 tablespoon Dijon mustard
- 1 tablespoon whole grain mustard
- 2 tablespoons honey
- 1 tablespoon soy sauce
- 1 tablespoon white wine vinegar or lemon juice
- 2 cloves garlic, minced
- 1 teaspoon fresh thyme leaves (or 1/2 teaspoon dried thyme)
- Salt and black pepper to taste
- Lemon wedges (for serving)
- Fresh parsley (for garnish, optional)

Instructions:

1. **Preheat Oven:**
   - Preheat your oven to 400°F (200°C).
2. **Prepare the Mustard Glaze:**
   - In a small bowl, whisk together Dijon mustard, whole grain mustard, honey, soy sauce, white wine vinegar (or lemon juice), minced garlic, and thyme. Adjust seasoning with salt and pepper to taste.
3. **Prepare the Salmon:**
   - Pat the salmon fillets dry with paper towels.
   - Rub each fillet with olive oil and season with salt and pepper.
4. **Glaze the Salmon:**
   - Place the salmon fillets on a baking sheet lined with parchment paper or lightly greased.
   - Brush a generous amount of the mustard glaze over each salmon fillet.
5. **Bake the Salmon:**
   - Bake in the preheated oven for 12-15 minutes, or until the salmon flakes easily with a fork. The glaze should be caramelized and slightly bubbly.
6. **Serve:**
   - Remove the salmon from the oven and let it rest for a few minutes.
   - Garnish with fresh parsley and serve with lemon wedges on the side.

Tips:

- For a more intense flavor, you can marinate the salmon in the mustard glaze for 30 minutes to 1 hour before baking.
- This dish pairs beautifully with roasted vegetables, steamed greens, or a light salad.

Enjoy your flavorful Irish Salmon with Mustard Glaze!

Chicken and Leek Pie

Ingredients:

For the Filling:

- 2 tablespoons olive oil or butter
- 1 large onion, finely chopped
- 2-3 leeks, white and light green parts only, sliced
- 2 cloves garlic, minced
- 2 cups cooked chicken, diced (preferably boneless, skinless)
- 1 cup frozen peas (or fresh if preferred)
- 1/4 cup all-purpose flour
- 1 cup chicken broth
- 1 cup milk or cream
- 1 tablespoon Dijon mustard
- 1 teaspoon dried thyme
- 1 teaspoon dried rosemary (optional)
- Salt and black pepper to taste

For the Pastry:

- 1 package (14 oz) of store-bought pie pastry or 1 recipe for homemade pie crust
- 1 large egg, beaten (for egg wash)

Instructions:

1. **Prepare the Filling:**
    - Heat olive oil or butter in a large skillet over medium heat.
    - Add the chopped onion and cook until softened, about 5 minutes.
    - Add the leeks and cook until they are tender and slightly caramelized, about 8-10 minutes.
    - Stir in the minced garlic and cook for an additional minute.
    - Add the diced chicken and frozen peas. Stir to combine.
2. **Make the Sauce:**
    - Sprinkle the flour over the chicken and leek mixture. Stir well to coat and cook for 2 minutes.
    - Gradually add the chicken broth and milk (or cream), stirring constantly to avoid lumps.
    - Bring the mixture to a simmer and cook until the sauce thickens, about 5 minutes.
    - Stir in Dijon mustard, thyme, and rosemary (if using). Season with salt and black pepper to taste.
    - Remove from heat and let the filling cool slightly.
3. **Assemble the Pie:**
    - Preheat your oven to 400°F (200°C).

- Roll out half of the pie pastry and fit it into a 9-inch pie dish or baking dish. Trim any excess pastry.
- Pour the chicken and leek filling into the pastry-lined dish.
- Roll out the remaining pastry and place it over the filling. Trim excess pastry and crimp the edges to seal. Cut a few slits in the top crust to allow steam to escape.
- Brush the top of the pie with the beaten egg to give it a golden finish.

4. **Bake the Pie:**
   - Place the pie on a baking sheet to catch any drips.
   - Bake in the preheated oven for 25-30 minutes, or until the crust is golden brown and the filling is bubbly.
5. **Serve:**
   - Let the pie cool for a few minutes before slicing. Serve warm.

Tips:

- For a richer filling, you can substitute some of the milk with cream or add a splash of white wine.
- You can use leftover roast chicken or rotisserie chicken for a quicker preparation.

Enjoy your delicious Chicken and Leek Pie!

Irish Breakfast Casserole

Ingredients:

- 8 slices of bread (preferably Irish soda bread or any hearty bread), cubed
- 1 lb sausage (Irish breakfast sausage or any sausage), casings removed
- 4-6 slices of bacon, chopped
- 1 large onion, chopped
- 1 cup mushrooms, sliced (optional)
- 1 cup grated cheddar cheese
- 6 large eggs
- 1 cup milk or cream
- 1/2 cup sour cream
- 1 tablespoon Dijon mustard
- 1 teaspoon dried thyme
- 1 teaspoon dried parsley
- Salt and black pepper to taste
- 1/4 cup chopped fresh chives (optional, for garnish)

Instructions:

1. **Preheat Oven:**
   - Preheat your oven to 375°F (190°C). Grease a 9x13-inch baking dish or similar-sized casserole dish.
2. **Cook the Sausage and Bacon:**
   - In a large skillet, cook the sausage over medium heat until browned and cooked through, breaking it up with a spoon as it cooks. Remove from the skillet and set aside.
   - In the same skillet, cook the chopped bacon until crispy. Remove with a slotted spoon and drain on paper towels.
3. **Cook the Vegetables:**
   - Drain excess fat from the skillet, leaving a small amount. Add the chopped onion and cook until softened, about 5 minutes. If using mushrooms, add them and cook until they release their moisture and become golden brown.
4. **Assemble the Casserole:**
   - In the prepared baking dish, layer the cubed bread evenly.
   - Sprinkle the cooked sausage, bacon, onions, and mushrooms (if using) over the bread.
   - Sprinkle grated cheddar cheese on top.
5. **Prepare the Egg Mixture:**
   - In a large bowl, whisk together the eggs, milk, sour cream, Dijon mustard, thyme, parsley, salt, and black pepper.
6. **Pour and Bake:**
   - Pour the egg mixture evenly over the bread and meat layers in the baking dish.
   - Press down gently to ensure the bread absorbs the egg mixture.
7. **Bake:**

- Bake in the preheated oven for 35-45 minutes, or until the casserole is set in the middle and the top is golden brown. A knife inserted into the center should come out clean.
8. **Serve:**
    - Let the casserole cool for a few minutes before slicing.
    - Garnish with chopped fresh chives if desired.

Tips:

- For added flavor, you can include other traditional breakfast ingredients such as black pudding or white pudding, cut into small pieces.
- This casserole can be assembled the night before and baked in the morning for an easy breakfast option.

Enjoy your hearty and delicious Irish Breakfast Casserole!

Grilled Corned Beef Sandwiches

Ingredients:

- 8 slices of rye bread (or your favorite bread)
- 1/2 lb corned beef, sliced (thinly)
- 1 cup sauerkraut, drained
- 1 cup Swiss cheese, sliced or shredded
- 1/4 cup Russian or Thousand Island dressing (plus more for serving)
- 2 tablespoons butter (for grilling)

Instructions:

1. **Prepare the Sandwiches:**
   - Lay out 4 slices of rye bread on a work surface.
   - Spread a layer of Russian or Thousand Island dressing on each slice of bread.
   - Layer the corned beef evenly over the dressing.
   - Spread the drained sauerkraut over the corned beef.
   - Top with Swiss cheese.
   - Place the remaining 4 slices of rye bread on top to form sandwiches.
2. **Grill the Sandwiches:**
   - Heat a large skillet or griddle over medium heat.
   - Spread butter on the outside of each sandwich.
   - Place the sandwiches in the skillet and cook for 3-4 minutes per side, or until the bread is golden brown and the cheese is melted.
   - Press down lightly with a spatula to ensure even grilling and to help the cheese melt thoroughly.
3. **Serve:**
   - Remove the sandwiches from the skillet and let them cool for a minute before slicing.
   - Serve with additional dressing on the side for dipping if desired.

Tips:

- For extra flavor, you can add a few slices of pickles or some freshly ground black pepper to the sandwiches before grilling.
- If you prefer a different cheese, such as provolone or cheddar, feel free to substitute based on your taste.

Enjoy your delicious and classic Grilled Corned Beef Sandwiches!

Guinness BBQ Ribs

Ingredients:

For the Ribs:

- 2 racks of baby back ribs (about 2 lbs each)
- Salt and black pepper to taste
- 1 tablespoon smoked paprika
- 1 tablespoon garlic powder
- 1 tablespoon onion powder
- 1 teaspoon cumin
- 1 teaspoon chili powder

For the Guinness BBQ Sauce:

- 1 cup Guinness stout
- 1 cup ketchup
- 1/2 cup brown sugar
- 1/4 cup apple cider vinegar
- 2 tablespoons Worcestershire sauce
- 2 tablespoons Dijon mustard
- 1 tablespoon soy sauce
- 2 cloves garlic, minced
- 1 teaspoon smoked paprika
- 1 teaspoon onion powder
- 1/2 teaspoon salt
- 1/4 teaspoon black pepper
- 1/4 teaspoon red pepper flakes (optional, for heat)

Instructions:

1. **Prepare the Ribs:**
    - Preheat your oven to 300°F (150°C).
    - Remove the membrane from the back of the ribs if not already done. This will help the seasoning and sauce penetrate the meat.
    - In a small bowl, mix together salt, black pepper, smoked paprika, garlic powder, onion powder, cumin, and chili powder.
    - Rub the spice mixture evenly over both sides of the ribs.
2. **Cook the Ribs:**
    - Place the ribs on a rack in a roasting pan, bone side down. Cover tightly with aluminum foil.
    - Bake in the preheated oven for 2.5 to 3 hours, or until the ribs are tender.
3. **Prepare the Guinness BBQ Sauce:**
    - While the ribs are baking, make the BBQ sauce. In a medium saucepan, combine Guinness stout, ketchup, brown sugar, apple cider vinegar, Worcestershire

sauce, Dijon mustard, soy sauce, minced garlic, smoked paprika, onion powder, salt, black pepper, and red pepper flakes (if using).
    - Bring to a simmer over medium heat, stirring occasionally.
    - Reduce the heat to low and let the sauce simmer for 15-20 minutes, or until it thickens to your desired consistency. Stir occasionally.
4. **Grill the Ribs:**
    - Preheat your grill to medium-high heat.
    - Remove the ribs from the oven and discard the foil.
    - Brush a generous amount of Guinness BBQ sauce over the ribs.
    - Place the ribs on the grill and cook for 5-7 minutes per side, basting with additional sauce and turning occasionally, until the ribs are caramelized and slightly charred.
5. **Serve:**
    - Remove the ribs from the grill and let them rest for a few minutes before slicing.
    - Serve with extra Guinness BBQ sauce on the side.

Tips:

- For a smoky flavor, consider using a smoker or adding wood chips to your grill.
- If you prefer a sweeter sauce, you can adjust the amount of brown sugar in the recipe.

Enjoy your flavorful and tender Guinness BBQ Ribs!

Potato and Onion Gratin

Ingredients:

- 4 large potatoes (such as Russet or Yukon Gold), peeled and thinly sliced
- 2 large onions, thinly sliced
- 2 cloves garlic, minced
- 2 tablespoons butter
- 2 tablespoons all-purpose flour
- 1 1/2 cups milk (whole milk or cream for richness)
- 1 cup grated cheddar cheese (or Gruyère for a more sophisticated flavor)
- 1/2 cup grated Parmesan cheese
- 1 teaspoon dried thyme
- 1 teaspoon dried rosemary (optional)
- Salt and black pepper to taste
- 1/4 teaspoon nutmeg (optional)
- Fresh parsley, chopped (for garnish)

Instructions:

1. **Preheat Oven:**
   - Preheat your oven to 375°F (190°C). Grease a 9x13-inch baking dish or a similar-sized ovenproof dish.
2. **Prepare the Onions:**
   - In a large skillet, melt 1 tablespoon of butter over medium heat.
   - Add the sliced onions and cook, stirring occasionally, until they are soft and caramelized, about 15-20 minutes.
   - Add minced garlic and cook for an additional 1-2 minutes. Remove from heat.
3. **Prepare the Sauce:**
   - In a saucepan, melt the remaining 1 tablespoon of butter over medium heat.
   - Stir in the flour and cook for 1-2 minutes to form a roux.
   - Gradually whisk in the milk, making sure to eliminate any lumps. Continue to cook, stirring constantly, until the mixture thickens and becomes smooth.
   - Stir in the grated cheddar cheese, Parmesan cheese, dried thyme, rosemary (if using), salt, black pepper, and nutmeg (if using). Continue stirring until the cheese is melted and the sauce is well combined.
4. **Assemble the Gratin:**
   - Layer half of the sliced potatoes in the bottom of the prepared baking dish.
   - Spread half of the caramelized onions over the potatoes.
   - Pour a portion of the cheese sauce over the onions and potatoes.
   - Repeat the layers with the remaining potatoes, onions, and cheese sauce.
5. **Bake the Gratin:**
   - Cover the baking dish with aluminum foil and bake in the preheated oven for 45 minutes.
   - Remove the foil and bake for an additional 15-20 minutes, or until the top is golden brown and the potatoes are tender when pierced with a fork.
6. **Serve:**

- - Let the gratin rest for a few minutes before serving.
  - Garnish with chopped fresh parsley if desired.

Tips:

- For extra flavor, you can add a layer of crispy breadcrumbs mixed with a bit of melted butter on top of the gratin before baking.
- This dish can be made ahead of time and reheated, though it is best enjoyed fresh from the oven.

Enjoy your creamy and delicious Potato and Onion Gratin!

Irish Stuffed Cabbage Rolls

Ingredients:

For the Cabbage Rolls:

- 1 large head of cabbage
- 1 lb ground beef
- 1/2 lb ground pork
- 1 cup cooked rice (white or brown)
- 1 large onion, finely chopped
- 2 cloves garlic, minced
- 1 cup grated carrot
- 1 cup breadcrumbs
- 1 egg
- 1 teaspoon dried thyme
- 1 teaspoon dried parsley
- Salt and black pepper to taste

For the Sauce:

- 2 cups tomato sauce
- 1 cup beef broth (or chicken broth)
- 2 tablespoons brown sugar
- 1 tablespoon Worcestershire sauce
- 1 tablespoon apple cider vinegar
- 1 teaspoon paprika
- 1/2 teaspoon dried oregano
- Salt and black pepper to taste

Instructions:

1. **Prepare the Cabbage:**
   - Bring a large pot of water to a boil. Carefully remove the core from the cabbage and place the whole head in the boiling water.
   - Boil for 5-7 minutes, or until the outer leaves are pliable. Remove the cabbage from the water and let it cool slightly. Gently peel off 12-14 leaves, being careful not to tear them.
2. **Prepare the Filling:**
   - In a large bowl, combine ground beef, ground pork, cooked rice, chopped onion, minced garlic, grated carrot, breadcrumbs, egg, dried thyme, dried parsley, salt, and black pepper. Mix until well combined.
3. **Assemble the Rolls:**
   - Place a cabbage leaf on a flat surface. Spoon a portion of the filling onto the center of the leaf.
   - Fold the sides of the leaf over the filling, then roll from the bottom to enclose the filling completely. Secure with toothpicks if needed.
   - Repeat with the remaining leaves and filling.
4. **Prepare the Sauce:**

- In a medium bowl, mix together tomato sauce, beef broth, brown sugar, Worcestershire sauce, apple cider vinegar, paprika, dried oregano, salt, and black pepper.
5. **Bake the Cabbage Rolls:**
    - Preheat your oven to 350°F (175°C).
    - Spread a small amount of sauce in the bottom of a large baking dish.
    - Place the cabbage rolls seam-side down in the baking dish.
    - Pour the remaining sauce over the cabbage rolls.
    - Cover the baking dish with aluminum foil and bake for 45-60 minutes, or until the rolls are cooked through and tender.
6. **Serve:**
    - Remove the cabbage rolls from the oven and let them rest for a few minutes before serving.
    - Garnish with additional fresh parsley if desired.

Tips:

- For a richer flavor, you can add a bit of smoked paprika or a splash of white wine to the sauce.
- If you have leftover filling, you can freeze it or use it as a meatloaf mix.

Enjoy your comforting and flavorful Irish Stuffed Cabbage Rolls!

Traditional Irish Roast Beef

Ingredients:

- 4-5 lbs beef rib roast or sirloin roast
- 3 tablespoons olive oil
- 4 cloves garlic, minced
- 2 tablespoons fresh rosemary, chopped (or 2 teaspoons dried rosemary)
- 2 tablespoons fresh thyme, chopped (or 2 teaspoons dried thyme)
- Salt and black pepper to taste
- 1 cup beef broth
- 1 cup red wine (optional, can use additional beef broth)
- 2 large carrots, peeled and cut into chunks
- 2 large onions, peeled and quartered
- 2-3 parsnips, peeled and cut into chunks (optional)
- 4-6 small potatoes, halved (optional)

Instructions:

1. **Prepare the Roast:**
    - Preheat your oven to 425°F (220°C).
    - Pat the beef roast dry with paper towels. This helps to get a good sear.
    - Rub the roast all over with olive oil, minced garlic, chopped rosemary, thyme, salt, and black pepper.
2. **Sear the Roast:**
    - Heat a large oven-proof skillet or roasting pan over medium-high heat.
    - Sear the beef roast on all sides until browned, about 3-4 minutes per side.
3. **Prepare the Vegetables:**
    - Arrange the carrots, onions, parsnips (if using), and potatoes (if using) around the roast in the roasting pan.
    - Drizzle with a bit of olive oil and season with salt and black pepper.
4. **Roast the Beef:**
    - Place the skillet or roasting pan in the preheated oven.
    - Roast for about 20 minutes at 425°F (220°C), then reduce the oven temperature to 350°F (175°C) and continue roasting.
    - Cooking times will vary depending on the size of the roast and desired doneness. As a general guideline, roast the beef for about 15-20 minutes per pound for medium-rare, 20-25 minutes per pound for medium, and longer for well-done.
    - Use a meat thermometer to check the internal temperature:
        - **Rare:** 125°F (52°C)
        - **Medium Rare:** 135°F (57°C)
        - **Medium:** 145°F (63°C)
        - **Medium Well:** 150°F (66°C)
        - **Well Done:** 160°F (71°C)
5. **Rest the Roast:**
    - Remove the roast from the oven and transfer it to a cutting board.
    - Tent the roast with aluminum foil and let it rest for at least 15-20 minutes before carving. This helps the juices redistribute throughout the meat.
6. **Make the Gravy (Optional):**

- While the roast is resting, you can make a simple gravy. Place the roasting pan on the stovetop over medium heat.
- Add the red wine (if using) and scrape up any browned bits from the bottom of the pan.
- Add beef broth and simmer until the sauce is reduced and thickened to your liking.
- For a thicker gravy, you can mix a tablespoon of flour or cornstarch with a little cold water and stir it into the simmering gravy.

7. **Serve:**
   - Slice the roast beef against the grain and serve with the roasted vegetables and gravy.

Tips:

- Letting the roast rest is crucial for juicy, tender meat.
- If you prefer a more herbaceous flavor, you can add additional herbs like sage or tarragon to the seasoning.

Enjoy your traditional Irish roast beef with all the classic trimmings!

Irish-Style Pork Chops

Ingredients:

- 4 bone-in pork chops (about 1-inch thick)
- Salt and black pepper to taste
- 2 tablespoons olive oil
- 1 large onion, thinly sliced
- 2 apples (such as Granny Smith or Braeburn), peeled, cored, and sliced
- 2 cloves garlic, minced
- 1 cup chicken broth
- 1/2 cup dry white wine (or additional chicken broth)
- 2 tablespoons Dijon mustard
- 1 tablespoon whole grain mustard
- 1 tablespoon brown sugar
- 1 teaspoon dried thyme
- 1/2 teaspoon dried rosemary (optional)
- 2 tablespoons chopped fresh parsley (for garnish)

Instructions:

1. **Prepare the Pork Chops:**
   - Season the pork chops on both sides with salt and black pepper.
2. **Sear the Pork Chops:**
   - Heat olive oil in a large skillet over medium-high heat.
   - Add the pork chops and sear for about 4-5 minutes per side, or until they are golden brown. Remove the pork chops from the skillet and set aside.
3. **Cook the Vegetables and Apples:**
   - In the same skillet, add the sliced onion and cook for about 5 minutes, or until softened and slightly caramelized.
   - Add the sliced apples and cook for another 3-4 minutes, until the apples begin to soften.
   - Stir in the minced garlic and cook for an additional minute.
4. **Make the Sauce:**
   - Add chicken broth, white wine (if using), Dijon mustard, whole grain mustard, brown sugar, dried thyme, and dried rosemary (if using) to the skillet.
   - Stir well to combine and scrape up any browned bits from the bottom of the skillet.
5. **Simmer the Pork Chops:**
   - Return the seared pork chops to the skillet, nestling them into the sauce.
   - Reduce heat to low, cover, and simmer for about 20-25 minutes, or until the pork chops are cooked through and tender. The internal temperature should reach 145°F (63°C).
6. **Finish and Serve:**
   - Remove the pork chops from the skillet and place them on a serving platter.
   - Continue to simmer the sauce for a few minutes if you want it to thicken slightly.
   - Spoon the apple-onion mixture and sauce over the pork chops.
   - Garnish with chopped fresh parsley.

Tips:

- For extra flavor, you can deglaze the skillet with a splash of apple cider or a bit more wine before adding the broth.
- This dish pairs well with mashed potatoes, rice, or a simple green vegetable like steamed broccoli.

Enjoy your flavorful Irish-Style Pork Chops with their sweet and savory apple sauce!

Lamb and Barley Soup

Ingredients:

- 1 lb lamb stew meat, cut into bite-sized cubes
- 2 tablespoons olive oil
- 1 large onion, chopped
- 2 cloves garlic, minced
- 2 large carrots, peeled and diced
- 2 celery stalks, diced
- 1 cup pearl barley
- 1 cup diced potatoes
- 1 cup diced tomatoes (canned or fresh)
- 6 cups beef or lamb broth (or water)
- 1 teaspoon dried thyme
- 1 teaspoon dried rosemary
- 1 bay leaf
- 1 cup frozen peas (optional)
- Salt and black pepper to taste
- Fresh parsley, chopped (for garnish)

Instructions:

1. **Brown the Lamb:**
   - Heat olive oil in a large pot or Dutch oven over medium-high heat.
   - Add the lamb cubes and cook, stirring occasionally, until browned on all sides. Remove the lamb from the pot and set aside.
2. **Sauté the Vegetables:**
   - In the same pot, add the chopped onion and cook until softened, about 5 minutes.
   - Add the minced garlic, carrots, and celery, and cook for another 5 minutes, stirring occasionally.
3. **Add Barley and Broth:**
   - Stir in the pearl barley and cook for 1-2 minutes.
   - Add the diced potatoes, diced tomatoes, beef or lamb broth, dried thyme, dried rosemary, and bay leaf.
   - Return the browned lamb to the pot and bring the mixture to a boil.
4. **Simmer the Soup:**
   - Reduce heat to low, cover, and let the soup simmer for about 45-60 minutes, or until the lamb is tender and the barley is cooked. Stir occasionally.
   - If using, add the frozen peas in the last 10 minutes of cooking.
5. **Season and Serve:**
   - Remove the bay leaf and discard.
   - Season the soup with salt and black pepper to taste.
   - Garnish with fresh chopped parsley before serving.

Tips:

- For added richness, you can use lamb stock if available.

- If you prefer a thicker soup, you can use a hand blender to partially puree the soup or mash some of the potatoes and barley against the side of the pot.
- This soup stores well in the refrigerator and often tastes even better the next day.

Enjoy your hearty and flavorful Lamb and Barley Soup!

Creamy Irish Potato Soup

Ingredients:

- 4 large potatoes (such as Russet or Yukon Gold), peeled and diced
- 1 large onion, chopped
- 2 cloves garlic, minced
- 3 tablespoons butter
- 1 large leek, cleaned and sliced (white and light green parts only)
- 4 cups chicken or vegetable broth
- 1 cup heavy cream (or half-and-half for a lighter option)
- 1/2 cup milk (optional, for additional creaminess)
- 1 teaspoon dried thyme
- 1 bay leaf
- Salt and black pepper to taste
- 1 cup shredded cheddar cheese (optional, for garnish)
- 2 tablespoons chopped fresh chives or parsley (for garnish)

Instructions:

1. **Prepare the Vegetables:**
   - In a large pot, melt the butter over medium heat.
   - Add the chopped onion, garlic, and sliced leek. Cook until the vegetables are softened, about 5-7 minutes.
2. **Cook the Potatoes:**
   - Add the diced potatoes to the pot and cook for an additional 5 minutes, stirring occasionally.
   - Pour in the chicken or vegetable broth and add the bay leaf and dried thyme.
   - Bring the mixture to a boil, then reduce heat and simmer until the potatoes are tender, about 15-20 minutes.
3. **Blend the Soup:**
   - Remove the bay leaf from the pot.
   - Using an immersion blender, blend the soup until smooth and creamy. Alternatively, you can transfer the soup in batches to a blender and blend until smooth. If using a blender, be sure to let the soup cool slightly and blend in batches to avoid splattering.
4. **Add Cream and Seasonings:**
   - Return the blended soup to the pot (if using a stand blender).
   - Stir in the heavy cream and milk (if using). Heat the soup over low heat until warmed through. Adjust the consistency by adding more milk if desired.
   - Season with salt and black pepper to taste.
5. **Serve:**
   - Ladle the soup into bowls.
   - Garnish with shredded cheddar cheese and chopped fresh chives or parsley, if desired.

Tips:

- For extra flavor, you can add a splash of white wine or a bit of crumbled bacon as a garnish.
- If you prefer a chunkier texture, blend only half of the soup and leave the rest as is.

Enjoy your creamy and comforting Irish Potato Soup!

Irish Cheddar Mac and Cheese

Ingredients:

For the Mac and Cheese:

- 12 oz (340 g) elbow macaroni (or any pasta shape you prefer)
- 2 tablespoons butter
- 2 tablespoons all-purpose flour
- 2 cups whole milk (or 2 cups half-and-half for extra creaminess)
- 2 cups shredded Irish cheddar cheese (or a mix of Irish cheddar and Gruyère for added depth)
- 1 cup grated Parmesan cheese
- 1/2 teaspoon Dijon mustard
- 1/2 teaspoon garlic powder
- 1/2 teaspoon onion powder
- Salt and black pepper to taste
- 1/4 teaspoon smoked paprika (optional, for a smoky flavor)

For the Topping (Optional):

- 1/2 cup panko breadcrumbs
- 2 tablespoons melted butter
- 1/4 cup shredded Irish cheddar cheese

Instructions:

1. **Cook the Pasta:**
   - Preheat your oven to 375°F (190°C).
   - Cook the elbow macaroni in a large pot of salted boiling water according to package instructions until al dente. Drain and set aside.
2. **Prepare the Cheese Sauce:**
   - In a large saucepan or skillet, melt the butter over medium heat.
   - Stir in the flour and cook for 1-2 minutes to form a roux, stirring constantly to prevent lumps.
   - Gradually whisk in the milk, continuing to stir until the mixture is smooth and begins to thicken, about 3-5 minutes.
   - Reduce the heat to low and stir in the shredded Irish cheddar cheese and grated Parmesan cheese until melted and smooth.
   - Add Dijon mustard, garlic powder, onion powder, smoked paprika (if using), salt, and black pepper. Taste and adjust seasoning as needed.
3. **Combine Pasta and Sauce:**
   - Add the cooked macaroni to the cheese sauce and stir until the pasta is evenly coated.
4. **Prepare the Topping (Optional):**
   - In a small bowl, mix together the panko breadcrumbs with melted butter.
   - Stir in the additional shredded Irish cheddar cheese.

5. **Bake the Mac and Cheese:**
   - Pour the macaroni and cheese mixture into a greased 9x13-inch baking dish or similarly-sized ovenproof dish.
   - Sprinkle the breadcrumb mixture evenly over the top.
6. **Bake:**
   - Bake in the preheated oven for 20-25 minutes, or until the top is golden brown and the cheese is bubbly.
7. **Serve:**
   - Let the mac and cheese rest for a few minutes before serving to allow it to set slightly.

Tips:

- For extra flavor, you can add cooked bacon, caramelized onions, or sautéed mushrooms to the mac and cheese.
- You can make this dish ahead of time and freeze it before baking. Just thaw and bake as directed when ready to serve.

Enjoy your creamy, cheesy, and delicious Irish Cheddar Mac and Cheese!

Potato and Leek Soup

Ingredients:

- 3 large leeks, white and light green parts only, cleaned and sliced
- 4 large potatoes (such as Yukon Gold or Russet), peeled and diced
- 2 tablespoons olive oil or butter
- 3 cloves garlic, minced
- 1 large onion, chopped
- 4 cups vegetable or chicken broth
- 1 cup water (or additional broth)
- 1 cup heavy cream (or half-and-half for a lighter option)
- 1 teaspoon dried thyme
- 1 bay leaf
- Salt and black pepper to taste
- Fresh chives or parsley, chopped (for garnish)
- Optional: Crumbled bacon or shredded cheddar cheese (for garnish)

Instructions:

1. **Prepare the Leeks:**
   - Slice the leeks and rinse them thoroughly to remove any dirt or sand. Leeks can trap grit between their layers, so make sure to rinse well.
2. **Sauté the Vegetables:**
   - In a large pot, heat olive oil or butter over medium heat.
   - Add the chopped onion and cook until softened, about 5 minutes.
   - Add the sliced leeks and cook for another 5 minutes, stirring occasionally, until they are tender.
3. **Add Potatoes and Garlic:**
   - Stir in the minced garlic and cook for 1 minute.
   - Add the diced potatoes and cook for another 5 minutes.
4. **Add Broth and Simmer:**
   - Pour in the vegetable or chicken broth and water.
   - Add dried thyme, bay leaf, salt, and black pepper.
   - Bring the mixture to a boil, then reduce the heat and let it simmer for about 20-25 minutes, or until the potatoes are tender.
5. **Blend the Soup:**
   - Remove the bay leaf.
   - Using an immersion blender, blend the soup until smooth and creamy. Alternatively, you can carefully transfer the soup in batches to a blender and blend until smooth. If using a blender, allow the soup to cool slightly and blend in batches to avoid splattering.
6. **Add Cream:**
   - Return the blended soup to the pot if using a stand blender.
   - Stir in the heavy cream and heat the soup over low heat until warmed through. Adjust seasoning with salt and pepper if needed.
7. **Serve:**

- Ladle the soup into bowls.
- Garnish with chopped fresh chives or parsley.
- Optionally, top with crumbled bacon or shredded cheddar cheese for added flavor.

Tips:

- For a richer flavor, use homemade broth if possible.
- If you prefer a chunkier texture, blend only half of the soup and leave the rest as is.

Enjoy your warm and creamy Potato and Leek Soup!

Braised Beef with Root Vegetables

Ingredients:

- 3-4 lbs beef chuck roast or braising beef, cut into large chunks
- Salt and black pepper to taste
- 2 tablespoons olive oil
- 1 large onion, chopped
- 3 cloves garlic, minced
- 4 carrots, peeled and cut into chunks
- 3 parsnips, peeled and cut into chunks (optional)
- 2 large potatoes, peeled and cut into chunks
- 2 cups beef broth (or more if needed)
- 1 cup red wine (optional, can use additional beef broth)
- 2 tablespoons tomato paste
- 1 tablespoon Worcestershire sauce
- 2 teaspoons dried thyme
- 1 teaspoon dried rosemary
- 1 bay leaf
- 1 tablespoon all-purpose flour (optional, for thickening)
- 2 tablespoons chopped fresh parsley (for garnish)

Instructions:

1. **Prepare the Beef:**
    - Season the beef chunks with salt and black pepper.
2. **Brown the Beef:**
    - Heat olive oil in a large Dutch oven or oven-safe pot over medium-high heat.
    - Add the beef chunks in batches, searing them on all sides until browned. Remove the browned beef and set aside.
3. **Sauté the Vegetables:**
    - In the same pot, add the chopped onion and cook until softened, about 5 minutes.
    - Add the minced garlic and cook for an additional 1 minute.
4. **Deglaze the Pot:**
    - Stir in the tomato paste and cook for 1-2 minutes until it begins to darken.
    - Pour in the red wine (if using) and scrape up any browned bits from the bottom of the pot.
5. **Add Broth and Seasonings:**
    - Return the browned beef to the pot.
    - Add the beef broth, Worcestershire sauce, dried thyme, dried rosemary, and bay leaf.
    - Stir to combine and bring the mixture to a simmer.
6. **Braised the Beef:**
    - Cover the pot with a lid and transfer it to a preheated oven at 325°F (165°C).
    - Braise the beef in the oven for 2.5 to 3 hours, or until the meat is tender and easily shreds with a fork.
7. **Add Vegetables:**

- About 45 minutes before the beef is done, add the carrots, parsnips (if using), and potatoes to the pot.
- Stir to combine and continue cooking until the vegetables are tender and the beef is fully cooked.

8. **Thicken the Sauce (Optional):**
    - If you prefer a thicker sauce, remove the beef and vegetables from the pot once cooked.
    - In a small bowl, mix 1 tablespoon of flour with a little cold water to form a slurry.
    - Stir the slurry into the simmering sauce and cook for a few minutes until thickened.
9. **Serve:**
    - Return the beef and vegetables to the pot if you removed them.
    - Garnish with chopped fresh parsley before serving.

Tips:

- For added depth of flavor, you can include additional ingredients like mushrooms or parsnips.
- This dish pairs well with crusty bread or mashed potatoes.

Enjoy your hearty and flavorful Braised Beef with Root Vegetables!

Irish Meatballs with Cabbage

Ingredients:

For the Meatballs:

- 1 lb ground beef
- 1/2 lb ground pork
- 1 cup fresh breadcrumbs (or dried breadcrumbs soaked in milk)
- 1/2 cup grated onion
- 1 large egg
- 2 cloves garlic, minced
- 1/4 cup fresh parsley, chopped
- 1 teaspoon dried thyme
- 1 teaspoon dried rosemary
- Salt and black pepper to taste

For the Cabbage:

- 1 medium head of cabbage, shredded
- 2 tablespoons olive oil
- 1 large onion, chopped
- 2 cloves garlic, minced
- 1/2 cup chicken broth (or beef broth)
- 1 tablespoon apple cider vinegar
- 1 tablespoon brown sugar (optional)
- Salt and black pepper to taste

Instructions:

1. **Prepare the Meatballs:**
    - Preheat your oven to 375°F (190°C).
    - In a large bowl, combine the ground beef, ground pork, breadcrumbs, grated onion, egg, minced garlic, chopped parsley, dried thyme, dried rosemary, salt, and black pepper.
    - Mix until all ingredients are well combined but don't overmix to keep the meatballs tender.
    - Form the mixture into 1 to 1.5-inch meatballs and place them on a baking sheet.
2. **Bake the Meatballs:**
    - Bake the meatballs in the preheated oven for 20-25 minutes, or until they are cooked through and browned on the outside. You can check for doneness with a meat thermometer; the internal temperature should reach 160°F (71°C).
3. **Prepare the Cabbage:**
    - While the meatballs are baking, heat olive oil in a large skillet over medium heat.
    - Add the chopped onion and cook until softened, about 5 minutes.
    - Add the minced garlic and cook for an additional 1 minute.
    - Stir in the shredded cabbage and cook, stirring occasionally, until the cabbage starts to wilt, about 5 minutes.
4. **Add Broth and Seasonings:**

- Pour in the chicken broth and add the apple cider vinegar. Stir to combine.
- If desired, add brown sugar to balance the flavors.
- Reduce heat to low, cover, and simmer for about 10-15 minutes, or until the cabbage is tender and the flavors are well combined. Season with salt and black pepper to taste.

5. **Combine and Serve:**
    - Once the meatballs are done baking, add them to the skillet with the cabbage.
    - Stir gently to combine and heat everything through.
    - Serve the meatballs and cabbage hot, garnished with additional fresh parsley if desired.

Tips:

- For extra flavor, you can add caraway seeds or a touch of paprika to the cabbage.
- If you prefer, you can make the meatballs ahead of time and freeze them. Reheat them in the sauce before serving.

Enjoy your flavorful and comforting Irish Meatballs with Cabbage!

Corned Beef Hash

Ingredients:

- 2 cups cooked corned beef, diced (leftover corned beef works great)
- 2 cups cooked potatoes, diced (peeled and boiled or baked potatoes, cooled)
- 1 large onion, finely chopped
- 2 cloves garlic, minced
- 2 tablespoons vegetable oil or butter
- 1 red bell pepper, diced (optional, for added color and flavor)
- 1/2 teaspoon dried thyme or rosemary
- Salt and black pepper to taste
- 2-4 large eggs (optional, for serving)
- Fresh parsley, chopped (for garnish)

Instructions:

1. **Prepare the Ingredients:**
   - If using leftover corned beef, shred or dice it into small pieces.
   - Dice the cooked potatoes into small cubes. If using raw potatoes, peel and cube them, then boil until tender, about 10-12 minutes, and drain.
2. **Cook the Onion and Garlic:**
   - Heat vegetable oil or butter in a large skillet over medium heat.
   - Add the chopped onion and cook until softened and translucent, about 5 minutes.
   - Add the minced garlic and cook for an additional 1 minute.
3. **Add the Corned Beef and Potatoes:**
   - Add the diced corned beef and cooked potatoes to the skillet.
   - If using, add the diced red bell pepper.
   - Sprinkle with dried thyme or rosemary, salt, and black pepper.
   - Cook the mixture, stirring occasionally, until the potatoes and corned beef are well combined and starting to crisp up, about 10-15 minutes. Press the mixture down with a spatula occasionally to encourage crisping.
4. **Optional: Add Eggs:**
   - If you'd like to add eggs, make a few wells in the hash mixture with a spatula.
   - Crack an egg into each well and cover the skillet with a lid.
   - Cook over low heat until the egg whites are set but the yolks are still runny, about 4-5 minutes. For firmer yolks, cook for an additional minute or two.
5. **Serve:**
   - Garnish the corned beef hash with fresh chopped parsley.
   - Serve hot, with eggs on top if desired.

Tips:

- For a crispier hash, let the mixture cook undisturbed for a few minutes before stirring, allowing it to form a crust on the bottom.
- You can also add other vegetables like mushrooms or green beans for extra flavor and nutrition.

Enjoy your hearty and flavorful Corned Beef Hash!

Shepherd's Pie with Sweet Potato Topping

Ingredients:

For the Meat Filling:

- 1 lb ground beef or lamb (or a combination)
- 1 large onion, chopped
- 2 cloves garlic, minced
- 1 large carrot, diced
- 1 cup frozen peas
- 1 cup frozen corn (optional)
- 2 tablespoons tomato paste
- 1 tablespoon Worcestershire sauce
- 1 teaspoon dried thyme
- 1 teaspoon dried rosemary
- 1/2 cup beef or chicken broth
- Salt and black pepper to taste

For the Sweet Potato Topping:

- 2 large sweet potatoes, peeled and cubed
- 2 tablespoons butter
- 1/4 cup milk (or cream for extra richness)
- Salt and black pepper to taste
- 1/4 teaspoon ground cinnamon (optional, for added warmth)
- 1/4 teaspoon ground nutmeg (optional)

Instructions:

1. **Prepare the Sweet Potato Topping:**
    - Place the cubed sweet potatoes in a large pot and cover with cold water.
    - Bring to a boil and cook until tender, about 15-20 minutes.
    - Drain the sweet potatoes and return them to the pot.
    - Add butter and milk. Mash the sweet potatoes until smooth and creamy. Season with salt, black pepper, ground cinnamon, and nutmeg if using. Set aside.
2. **Cook the Meat Filling:**
    - Preheat your oven to 400°F (200°C).
    - In a large skillet, cook the ground beef or lamb over medium heat until browned. Drain any excess fat.
    - Add the chopped onion and cook until softened, about 5 minutes.
    - Stir in the minced garlic and cook for an additional 1 minute.
    - Add the diced carrot, frozen peas, and frozen corn (if using). Cook for another 5 minutes.
    - Stir in the tomato paste, Worcestershire sauce, dried thyme, and dried rosemary. Cook for 1-2 minutes.
    - Pour in the beef or chicken broth and bring to a simmer. Let it cook for about 5 minutes, or until the mixture thickens slightly. Season with salt and black pepper to taste.
3. **Assemble the Shepherd's Pie:**

- Transfer the meat filling to a 9x13-inch baking dish or a similar-sized ovenproof dish.
- Spread the sweet potato topping evenly over the meat filling, smoothing it out with a spatula. You can create a decorative pattern with a fork if desired.

4. **Bake:**
   - Place the baking dish in the preheated oven and bake for 20-25 minutes, or until the topping is slightly golden and the filling is bubbling.
5. **Serve:**
   - Let the Shepherd's Pie cool for a few minutes before serving.

Tips:

- You can prepare the meat filling and sweet potato topping ahead of time. Assemble and bake just before serving.
- For added flavor, you can sprinkle some shredded cheese on top of the sweet potato layer before baking.

Enjoy your delicious and comforting Shepherd's Pie with Sweet Potato Topping!

Guinness Braised Short Ribs

Ingredients:

- 4-5 lbs beef short ribs (bone-in)
- Salt and black pepper to taste

- 2 tablespoons vegetable oil
- 1 large onion, chopped
- 3 cloves garlic, minced
- 2 large carrots, peeled and sliced
- 2 celery stalks, sliced
- 2 tablespoons tomato paste
- 1 cup Guinness stout beer
- 2 cups beef broth
- 2 tablespoons Worcestershire sauce
- 1 teaspoon dried thyme
- 1 teaspoon dried rosemary
- 2 bay leaves
- 1 tablespoon all-purpose flour (optional, for thickening)
- 2 tablespoons chopped fresh parsley (for garnish)

Instructions:

1. **Prepare the Short Ribs:**
    - Preheat your oven to 325°F (165°C).
    - Season the beef short ribs generously with salt and black pepper.
2. **Brown the Short Ribs:**
    - Heat vegetable oil in a large Dutch oven or ovenproof pot over medium-high heat.
    - Add the short ribs in batches, browning them on all sides. Remove the browned ribs and set aside.
3. **Cook the Vegetables:**
    - In the same pot, add the chopped onion, carrots, and celery. Cook until the vegetables are softened, about 5-7 minutes.
    - Stir in the minced garlic and cook for an additional 1 minute.
    - Add the tomato paste and cook for 1-2 minutes, stirring to combine.
4. **Deglaze the Pot:**
    - Pour in the Guinness stout beer and scrape up any browned bits from the bottom of the pot.
5. **Add Broth and Seasonings:**
    - Return the browned short ribs to the pot.
    - Add the beef broth, Worcestershire sauce, dried thyme, dried rosemary, and bay leaves.
    - Bring the mixture to a boil, then reduce the heat to low.
6. **Braised the Short Ribs:**
    - Cover the pot with a lid and transfer it to the preheated oven.
    - Braise the short ribs in the oven for 2.5 to 3 hours, or until the meat is tender and falling off the bone.
7. **Optional: Thicken the Sauce:**
    - If you prefer a thicker sauce, remove the short ribs from the pot once they are cooked.

- On the stovetop, bring the sauce to a simmer and stir in a slurry made from 1 tablespoon of all-purpose flour mixed with a little water.
- Cook for a few minutes until the sauce has thickened.
8. **Serve:**
    - Return the short ribs to the pot, coat with the sauce, and heat through.
    - Garnish with chopped fresh parsley before serving.

Tips:

- For extra flavor, you can add a splash of balsamic vinegar or a spoonful of Dijon mustard to the sauce.
- Serve the short ribs with mashed potatoes, creamy polenta, or crusty bread to soak up the rich sauce.

Enjoy your hearty and flavorful Guinness Braised Short Ribs!

Irish Chicken Stew

Ingredients:

- 2 lbs bone-in, skinless chicken thighs or breasts (about 4-6 pieces), trimmed
- Salt and black pepper to taste

- 2 tablespoons olive oil or butter
- 1 large onion, chopped
- 3 cloves garlic, minced
- 4 large carrots, peeled and sliced
- 3 parsnips, peeled and sliced (optional)
- 2 large potatoes, peeled and cubed
- 1 cup frozen peas
- 4 cups chicken broth
- 1 cup white wine or additional chicken broth (optional)
- 2 tablespoons tomato paste
- 1 teaspoon dried thyme
- 1 teaspoon dried rosemary
- 2 bay leaves
- 1 tablespoon chopped fresh parsley (for garnish)
- 1 tablespoon cornstarch mixed with 2 tablespoons water (optional, for thickening)

Instructions:

1. **Prepare the Chicken:**
   - Season the chicken pieces with salt and black pepper.
2. **Brown the Chicken:**
   - In a large pot or Dutch oven, heat olive oil or butter over medium-high heat.
   - Add the chicken pieces and brown on all sides, about 5-7 minutes. Remove the chicken and set aside.
3. **Cook the Vegetables:**
   - In the same pot, add the chopped onion and cook until softened, about 5 minutes.
   - Add the minced garlic and cook for an additional 1 minute.
   - Stir in the sliced carrots, parsnips (if using), and cubed potatoes. Cook for 5 minutes.
4. **Add Tomato Paste and Deglaze:**
   - Stir in the tomato paste and cook for 1-2 minutes.
   - Pour in the white wine (if using) and scrape up any browned bits from the bottom of the pot.
5. **Add Broth and Seasonings:**
   - Return the browned chicken to the pot.
   - Add the chicken broth, dried thyme, dried rosemary, and bay leaves.
   - Bring the mixture to a boil, then reduce the heat to low and cover.
6. **Simmer the Stew:**
   - Let the stew simmer for 30-40 minutes, or until the chicken is cooked through and the vegetables are tender.
   - Remove the chicken from the pot and shred it into bite-sized pieces. Return the shredded chicken to the pot.
7. **Add Peas and Thicken (Optional):**
   - Stir in the frozen peas and cook for an additional 5 minutes.

- If you prefer a thicker stew, stir in the cornstarch slurry (cornstarch mixed with water) and cook for a few more minutes until the stew thickens.
8. **Serve:**
    - Remove the bay leaves from the stew.
    - Garnish with chopped fresh parsley before serving.

Tips:

- For extra flavor, you can add a splash of cream or a dollop of sour cream just before serving.
- You can also add other vegetables like turnips or green beans for variation.

Enjoy your hearty and comforting Irish Chicken Stew!

Irish Seafood Chowder

Ingredients:

- 2 tablespoons butter
- 1 large onion, chopped

- 2 cloves garlic, minced
- 2 large carrots, peeled and diced
- 2 celery stalks, diced
- 1 cup diced potatoes (peeled)
- 1 cup frozen or fresh corn kernels (optional)
- 4 cups fish stock or chicken broth
- 1 cup heavy cream (or half-and-half for a lighter option)
- 1 cup milk
- 1 cup diced white fish (such as cod, haddock, or pollock)
- 1 cup cooked shrimp (peeled and deveined)
- 1 cup diced mussels or clams (fresh or canned, drained)
- 1 teaspoon dried thyme
- 1 teaspoon dried dill
- 1 bay leaf
- Salt and black pepper to taste
- 2 tablespoons all-purpose flour (optional, for thickening)
- 2 tablespoons chopped fresh parsley (for garnish)
- Lemon wedges (for serving)

Instructions:

1. **Prepare the Vegetables:**
    - In a large pot or Dutch oven, melt the butter over medium heat.
    - Add the chopped onion and cook until softened, about 5 minutes.
    - Add the minced garlic and cook for an additional 1 minute.
2. **Cook the Vegetables:**
    - Stir in the diced carrots, celery, and potatoes. Cook for 5-7 minutes, stirring occasionally, until the vegetables begin to soften.
3. **Add the Broth:**
    - Pour in the fish stock or chicken broth and bring to a boil.
    - Reduce the heat and let it simmer for about 15 minutes, or until the potatoes and carrots are tender.
4. **Add Cream and Seasonings:**
    - Stir in the heavy cream and milk.
    - Add the dried thyme, dried dill, bay leaf, salt, and black pepper.
    - Bring the mixture back to a simmer.
5. **Add the Seafood:**
    - Gently add the diced white fish, cooked shrimp, and diced mussels or clams.
    - Simmer for an additional 5-7 minutes, or until the seafood is cooked through and the flavors are well combined.
6. **Optional: Thicken the Chowder:**
    - If you prefer a thicker chowder, mix 2 tablespoons of all-purpose flour with a little cold water to form a slurry.
    - Stir the slurry into the chowder and cook for a few more minutes until thickened.
7. **Serve:**

- Remove the bay leaf from the chowder.
- Garnish with chopped fresh parsley before serving.
- Serve hot with lemon wedges on the side and crusty bread or soda bread.

Tips:

- Use a variety of seafood for a more complex flavor. You can also add scallops or other shellfish if desired.
- For extra richness, you can add a splash of white wine to the broth.

Enjoy your creamy and delicious Irish Seafood Chowder!

Stuffed Shepherd's Pie

Ingredients:

For the Meat Filling:

- 1 lb ground beef or lamb (or a combination)

- 1 large onion, chopped
- 2 cloves garlic, minced
- 1 large carrot, diced
- 1 cup frozen peas
- 1 cup frozen corn (optional)
- 2 tablespoons tomato paste
- 1 tablespoon Worcestershire sauce
- 1 teaspoon dried thyme
- 1 teaspoon dried rosemary
- 1/2 cup beef broth
- Salt and black pepper to taste

For the Mashed Potato Topping:

- 4 large potatoes, peeled and cubed
- 4 tablespoons butter
- 1/2 cup milk (or cream for extra richness)
- Salt and black pepper to taste
- 1 cup shredded cheddar cheese (optional, for mixing into potatoes)

For the Stuffing:

- 1/2 cup shredded cheddar cheese (or cheese of your choice)
- 1/4 cup finely chopped fresh parsley (optional)

Instructions:

1. **Prepare the Meat Filling:**
   - Preheat your oven to 375°F (190°C).
   - In a large skillet, cook the ground beef or lamb over medium-high heat until browned. Drain any excess fat.
   - Add the chopped onion and cook until softened, about 5 minutes.
   - Stir in the minced garlic and cook for 1 minute.
   - Add the diced carrot, frozen peas, and frozen corn (if using). Cook for 5 minutes.
   - Stir in the tomato paste, Worcestershire sauce, dried thyme, and dried rosemary. Cook for 1-2 minutes.
   - Pour in the beef broth and simmer until the mixture thickens slightly. Season with salt and black pepper to taste. Remove from heat and set aside.
2. **Prepare the Mashed Potatoes:**
   - In a large pot, cover the cubed potatoes with cold water. Bring to a boil and cook until tender, about 15 minutes.
   - Drain the potatoes and return them to the pot.
   - Add the butter and milk (or cream) and mash until smooth and creamy. Season with salt and black pepper.
   - For a cheesy topping, mix in the shredded cheddar cheese if desired.

3. **Assemble the Stuffed Shepherd's Pie:**
   - Transfer half of the mashed potatoes to the bottom of a 9x13-inch baking dish or similar-sized ovenproof dish. Spread it out to form an even layer.
   - Sprinkle the 1/2 cup shredded cheddar cheese over the potato layer.
   - Carefully spread the meat filling over the cheese layer.
   - Top the meat filling with the remaining mashed potatoes, smoothing it out with a spatula.
4. **Bake:**
   - Place the baking dish in the preheated oven and bake for 25-30 minutes, or until the top is golden brown and the filling is bubbly.
5. **Garnish and Serve:**
   - If desired, garnish with finely chopped fresh parsley before serving.

Tips:

- For extra flavor, you can add sautéed mushrooms or a splash of red wine to the meat filling.
- Make sure the mashed potatoes are thick enough to hold their shape. If they're too runny, they may not hold up well during baking.

Enjoy your comforting and delicious Stuffed Shepherd's Pie!

Irish Brown Bread

Ingredients:

- 2 cups (250g) wholemeal flour (whole wheat flour)
- 1 cup (125g) all-purpose flour

- 1 teaspoon baking soda
- 1/2 teaspoon salt
- 1/4 cup (50g) brown sugar (optional, for a touch of sweetness)
- 2 tablespoons unsalted butter, softened (optional, for a richer texture)
- 1 1/2 cups (350ml) buttermilk (or milk with a splash of lemon juice or vinegar as a substitute)

Instructions:

1. **Preheat the Oven:**
   - Preheat your oven to 425°F (220°C). Grease or line a 9-inch round cake pan or a loaf pan with parchment paper.
2. **Mix the Dry Ingredients:**
   - In a large bowl, whisk together the wholemeal flour, all-purpose flour, baking soda, salt, and brown sugar (if using). If you're adding butter, cut it into the flour mixture using a pastry cutter or your fingers until it resembles coarse crumbs.
3. **Add the Buttermilk:**
   - Make a well in the center of the dry ingredients. Pour in the buttermilk and gently mix with a wooden spoon or your hands until the dough comes together. Be careful not to overmix; the dough should be slightly shaggy.
4. **Shape the Dough:**
   - Turn the dough out onto a floured surface and gently shape it into a round loaf or shape it to fit the loaf pan. If you're making a round loaf, flatten it slightly.
5. **Score the Bread:**
   - Using a sharp knife, score an "X" on the top of the loaf. This helps the bread cook evenly and gives it a traditional look.
6. **Bake:**
   - Place the loaf in the preheated oven and bake for 35-45 minutes, or until the bread sounds hollow when tapped on the bottom and is golden brown on top. The internal temperature should reach about 190°F (90°C).
7. **Cool:**
   - Remove the bread from the oven and let it cool on a wire rack before slicing.

Tips:

- **Buttermilk Substitute:** If you don't have buttermilk, you can use milk mixed with 1 tablespoon of lemon juice or white vinegar. Let it sit for 5 minutes before using.
- **Add-Ins:** You can enhance the bread by adding ingredients like sunflower seeds, oats, or dried fruits.
- **Storage:** Store the bread in an airtight container or wrapped in a clean cloth to keep it fresh. It's best enjoyed within a few days, but it can also be frozen for longer storage.

Enjoy your authentic and hearty Irish Brown Bread with a slather of butter or alongside your favorite stew!

Irish Herb Roasted Chicken

Ingredients:

- 1 whole chicken (about 4-5 lbs), patted dry
- Salt and black pepper to taste

- 2 tablespoons olive oil or melted butter
- 4 cloves garlic, minced
- 1 lemon, cut into wedges
- 1 small bunch of fresh thyme (about 6-8 sprigs)
- 1 small bunch of fresh rosemary (about 6-8 sprigs)
- 1 small bunch of fresh parsley (for garnish)
- 1 onion, quartered
- 2 carrots, peeled and cut into chunks
- 2 celery stalks, cut into chunks

For the Optional Glaze (for extra flavor):

- 2 tablespoons honey
- 1 tablespoon Dijon mustard

Instructions:

1. **Preheat the Oven:**
   - Preheat your oven to 425°F (220°C).
2. **Prepare the Chicken:**
   - Remove any giblets from the chicken cavity. Pat the chicken dry with paper towels.
3. **Season the Chicken:**
   - Rub the chicken inside and out with olive oil or melted butter.
   - Season generously with salt and black pepper.
   - Rub minced garlic all over the chicken.
4. **Stuff the Chicken:**
   - Stuff the cavity with lemon wedges, a few sprigs of thyme, rosemary, and parsley.
5. **Prepare the Vegetables:**
   - Place the onion, carrots, and celery in the bottom of a roasting pan. These will act as a bed for the chicken and add flavor to the drippings.
6. **Roast the Chicken:**
   - Place the chicken, breast-side up, on top of the vegetables in the roasting pan.
   - If using, mix the honey and Dijon mustard to create a glaze. Brush this mixture over the chicken for a caramelized finish.
   - Roast in the preheated oven for about 1 hour and 15 minutes, or until the internal temperature reaches 165°F (74°C) in the thickest part of the thigh. The skin should be golden brown and crispy.
7. **Rest the Chicken:**
   - Once the chicken is done, remove it from the oven and let it rest for 15 minutes before carving. This allows the juices to redistribute, making the chicken more tender and flavorful.
8. **Serve:**
   - Carve the chicken and serve with the roasted vegetables and any other side dishes of your choice. Garnish with additional fresh parsley if desired.

Tips:

- **Basting:** For extra juicy chicken, you can baste it with the pan juices halfway through cooking.
- **Crispier Skin:** If you prefer a crispier skin, increase the oven temperature to 450°F (230°C) for the last 10 minutes of roasting, but keep an eye on it to prevent burning.
- **Gravy:** Use the pan drippings to make a delicious gravy. Simply whisk in some flour to the drippings, cook until golden, and then add a bit of chicken broth.

Enjoy your flavorful and aromatic Irish Herb Roasted Chicken!

Beef and Ale Pie

Ingredients:

For the Filling:

- 2 lbs (900g) beef chuck or stewing beef, cut into 1-inch cubes

- Salt and black pepper to taste
- 2 tablespoons vegetable oil
- 1 large onion, chopped
- 2 cloves garlic, minced
- 2 large carrots, peeled and diced
- 2 celery stalks, diced
- 2 tablespoons tomato paste
- 2 tablespoons all-purpose flour
- 1 cup (240ml) brown ale or stout (such as Guinness)
- 2 cups (480ml) beef broth
- 1 tablespoon Worcestershire sauce
- 1 teaspoon dried thyme
- 1 teaspoon dried rosemary
- 1 bay leaf
- 1 cup frozen peas
- 1 cup diced mushrooms (optional)

For the Pastry:

- 2 1/2 cups (315g) all-purpose flour
- 1/2 teaspoon salt
- 1 cup (225g) unsalted butter, cold and cut into small cubes
- 6-8 tablespoons ice water

For Assembly:

- 1 egg, beaten (for egg wash)
- Fresh thyme or rosemary for garnish (optional)

Instructions:

1. **Prepare the Filling:**
   - Season the beef cubes with salt and black pepper.
   - Heat vegetable oil in a large pot or Dutch oven over medium-high heat.
   - Add the beef in batches, browning on all sides. Remove the beef and set aside.
   - In the same pot, add the chopped onion, carrots, and celery. Cook until softened, about 5 minutes.
   - Stir in the minced garlic and cook for 1 minute.
   - Add the tomato paste and cook for 2 minutes.
   - Sprinkle the flour over the vegetables and stir to coat. Cook for 1-2 minutes.
   - Pour in the ale and beef broth, scraping up any browned bits from the bottom of the pot.
   - Return the beef to the pot and add Worcestershire sauce, dried thyme, dried rosemary, and bay leaf.

- Bring the mixture to a boil, then reduce the heat to low and cover. Simmer for 1.5 to 2 hours, or until the beef is tender.
- Stir in the frozen peas and diced mushrooms (if using) and cook for an additional 5 minutes. Remove the bay leaf. Adjust seasoning with salt and pepper if needed. Let the filling cool slightly.

2. **Prepare the Pastry:**
   - In a large bowl, combine the flour and salt.
   - Cut in the cold butter using a pastry cutter or your fingers until the mixture resembles coarse crumbs.
   - Gradually add ice water, 1 tablespoon at a time, mixing until the dough just comes together. Be careful not to overwork it.
   - Divide the dough into two portions, one slightly larger for the base and one for the top. Flatten each portion into discs and wrap in plastic wrap. Refrigerate for at least 30 minutes.

3. **Assemble the Pie:**
   - Preheat your oven to 375°F (190°C).
   - Roll out the larger dough portion on a floured surface to fit a 9-inch pie dish. Place the dough into the dish, pressing it into the corners.
   - Spoon the beef filling into the pie crust, smoothing it out.
   - Roll out the remaining dough portion and place it over the filling. Trim any excess dough and crimp the edges to seal. Cut a few slits in the top crust to allow steam to escape.
   - Brush the top crust with the beaten egg for a golden finish.

4. **Bake:**
   - Place the pie on a baking sheet to catch any drips and bake for 45-50 minutes, or until the crust is golden brown and the filling is bubbling.

5. **Serve:**
   - Let the pie cool for a few minutes before serving. Garnish with fresh thyme or rosemary if desired.

Tips:

- **Make Ahead:** You can prepare the filling a day in advance and store it in the refrigerator. Assemble and bake the pie on the day you plan to serve it.
- **Crust Variations:** For a shortcut, you can use store-bought pie crusts if you prefer.

Enjoy your hearty and flavorful Beef and Ale Pie!

Irish Caramelized Onion Soup

Ingredients:

- 4 large onions, thinly sliced

- 3 tablespoons butter
- 2 tablespoons olive oil
- 2 cloves garlic, minced
- 1 teaspoon sugar (optional, to aid in caramelizing)
- 1 teaspoon fresh thyme leaves (or 1/2 teaspoon dried thyme)
- 1 bay leaf
- 4 cups beef broth (or vegetable broth for a lighter version)
- 1 cup white wine (or additional broth)
- 1 tablespoon all-purpose flour (optional, for thickening)
- Salt and black pepper to taste
- 1 baguette, sliced
- 1 1/2 cups shredded Gruyère cheese (or Swiss cheese)

Instructions:

1. **Caramelize the Onions:**
    - In a large pot or Dutch oven, heat the butter and olive oil over medium heat.
    - Add the sliced onions and a pinch of salt. Cook, stirring frequently, for about 30-40 minutes, or until the onions are deep golden brown and caramelized. You may need to adjust the heat to prevent burning and add the sugar if you want a deeper caramelization.
    - Stir in the minced garlic and cook for an additional 1 minute.
2. **Add Herbs and Broth:**
    - Add the fresh thyme, bay leaf, and flour (if using) to the onions. Cook for 1-2 minutes to coat the onions and cook out the raw flour taste.
    - Pour in the white wine and cook for 2-3 minutes, scraping up any browned bits from the bottom of the pot.
    - Add the beef broth and bring the soup to a simmer. Reduce the heat and let it cook for 20 minutes to blend the flavors. Season with salt and black pepper to taste. Remove the bay leaf.
3. **Prepare the Bread and Cheese:**
    - While the soup is simmering, preheat your broiler.
    - Place the baguette slices on a baking sheet and toast under the broiler until golden brown on both sides. You may also rub the toasted bread with a cut clove of garlic for extra flavor.
4. **Assemble and Broil:**
    - Ladle the soup into ovenproof bowls or ramekins. Place the toasted baguette slices on top of the soup and sprinkle generously with shredded Gruyère cheese.
    - Place the bowls under the broiler for a few minutes, until the cheese is melted and bubbly, and starts to turn golden brown.
5. **Serve:**
    - Carefully remove the bowls from the oven and let them cool slightly before serving.

Tips:

- **Caramelization Time:** Be patient with caramelizing the onions; it's key to developing the rich, sweet flavor. If the onions start to brown too quickly, reduce the heat and continue cooking slowly.
- **Wine Substitute:** If you prefer not to use wine, you can substitute it with additional broth or a splash of sherry or brandy.

Enjoy your hearty and flavorful Irish Caramelized Onion Soup!

Dublin Bay Prawns with Garlic Butter

Ingredients:

- 1 lb (450g) Dublin Bay prawns (or langoustines/scampi), thawed if frozen
- 4 tablespoons unsalted butter

- 4 cloves garlic, minced
- 2 tablespoons olive oil
- 1 tablespoon fresh lemon juice
- 1/4 cup fresh parsley, finely chopped
- Salt and black pepper to taste
- Lemon wedges for serving

Instructions:

1. **Prepare the Prawns:**
   - If the prawns are not pre-cooked, you'll need to cook them first. Bring a large pot of salted water to a boil. Add the prawns and cook for 2-3 minutes, until they turn pink and are cooked through. Drain and let them cool slightly. Peel and devein if necessary.
2. **Prepare the Garlic Butter:**
   - In a large skillet, heat the olive oil and butter over medium heat until the butter is melted.
   - Add the minced garlic and cook for about 1-2 minutes, or until fragrant. Be careful not to burn the garlic.
3. **Add the Prawns:**
   - Add the cooked prawns to the skillet with the garlic butter. Toss to coat the prawns evenly with the butter and garlic.
   - Cook for an additional 2-3 minutes, just until the prawns are heated through and well-coated with the butter mixture.
4. **Add Lemon Juice and Parsley:**
   - Stir in the lemon juice and chopped parsley. Season with salt and black pepper to taste. Toss everything to combine.
5. **Serve:**
   - Transfer the prawns to a serving platter. Serve immediately with lemon wedges on the side for squeezing over the prawns.

Tips:

- **Prawns:** If using pre-cooked prawns, reduce the cooking time and just heat them through to avoid overcooking.
- **Butter:** For extra richness, you can use a combination of butter and a splash of white wine or a bit of cream in the garlic butter.
- **Side Dish:** Serve the prawns with crusty bread to soak up the delicious garlic butter, or alongside a fresh salad.

Enjoy your flavorful and succulent Dublin Bay Prawns with Garlic Butter!

Corned Beef Tacos

Ingredients:

For the Corned Beef:

- 2 cups cooked corned beef, shredded or chopped
- 1 tablespoon olive oil
- 1 small onion, finely chopped
- 2 cloves garlic, minced
- 1 teaspoon ground cumin
- 1 teaspoon smoked paprika
- 1/2 teaspoon chili powder
- Salt and black pepper to taste

For the Tacos:

- 8 small tortillas (corn or flour)
- 1 cup shredded lettuce
- 1 cup diced tomatoes
- 1/2 cup finely chopped red onion
- 1 avocado, sliced
- 1/2 cup sour cream
- 1/2 cup shredded cheddar cheese
- 1/4 cup chopped fresh cilantro
- Lime wedges (for serving)
- Hot sauce (optional)

Instructions:

1. **Prepare the Corned Beef:**
    - Heat olive oil in a skillet over medium heat.
    - Add the chopped onion and cook until softened, about 3-4 minutes.
    - Add the minced garlic and cook for an additional 1 minute.
    - Stir in the shredded or chopped corned beef, cumin, smoked paprika, chili powder, salt, and black pepper. Cook, stirring occasionally, until the corned beef is heated through and well-coated with the spices, about 5-7 minutes.
2. **Warm the Tortillas:**
    - Heat the tortillas in a dry skillet over medium heat for about 30 seconds on each side, or until warm and pliable. Alternatively, you can wrap them in foil and warm them in the oven.
3. **Assemble the Tacos:**
    - Spread a small amount of the corned beef mixture onto each tortilla.
    - Top with shredded lettuce, diced tomatoes, chopped red onion, avocado slices, and shredded cheddar cheese.
    - Dollop with sour cream and sprinkle with chopped fresh cilantro.
4. **Serve:**
    - Serve the tacos with lime wedges and hot sauce on the side, allowing everyone to customize their tacos to taste.

Tips:

- **Corned Beef:** Use leftover corned beef or store-bought corned beef for convenience. If using leftover corned beef, make sure it is reheated thoroughly.
- **Add-Ins:** Feel free to add other toppings like pickled jalapeños, black beans, or corn for extra flavor and texture.
- **Spice Level:** Adjust the amount of chili powder and hot sauce to control the spice level according to your preference.

Enjoy your creative and flavorful Corned Beef Tacos!

Irish Lamb Chops with Mint Jelly

Ingredients:

For the Lamb Chops:

- 8 lamb chops (about 1 inch thick)

- Salt and black pepper to taste
- 2 tablespoons olive oil
- 3 cloves garlic, minced
- 1 tablespoon fresh rosemary leaves (or 1 teaspoon dried rosemary)
- 1 tablespoon fresh thyme leaves (or 1 teaspoon dried thyme)

For the Mint Jelly:

- 1 cup fresh mint leaves, chopped
- 1 cup sugar
- 1 cup water
- 1 tablespoon lemon juice
- 1 tablespoon white vinegar
- 1 packet (1.75 oz) fruit pectin (such as Certo)

Instructions:

1. **Prepare the Mint Jelly:**
   - In a medium saucepan, combine the chopped mint leaves, sugar, and water. Bring to a boil over medium heat, stirring constantly until the sugar is dissolved.
   - Reduce heat and simmer for 5 minutes.
   - Stir in the lemon juice and white vinegar.
   - Add the fruit pectin and continue to stir for 1-2 minutes until well combined.
   - Remove from heat and let the mixture cool slightly.
   - Pour the mint jelly into sterilized jars and allow it to set. It will thicken as it cools. Store in the refrigerator until ready to use.
2. **Prepare the Lamb Chops:**
   - Preheat your grill or oven to medium-high heat (about 375°F or 190°C).
   - Season the lamb chops with salt and black pepper. Rub them with olive oil, minced garlic, rosemary, and thyme.
   - If grilling, place the lamb chops on the grill and cook for 4-5 minutes per side for medium-rare, or until they reach your desired level of doneness. If baking, place the lamb chops on a baking sheet and bake for about 15-20 minutes, turning halfway through, or until cooked to your liking.
3. **Serve:**
   - Remove the lamb chops from the grill or oven and let them rest for a few minutes.
   - Serve the lamb chops with a dollop of mint jelly on the side or drizzled over the top.

Tips:

- **Doneness:** Use a meat thermometer to check the internal temperature of the lamb chops. For medium-rare, it should be around 135°F (57°C). For medium, aim for 145°F (63°C).

- **Mint Jelly Variations:** For a more pronounced mint flavor, you can add extra mint leaves or a splash of mint extract.
- **Accompaniments:** Serve with traditional Irish sides such as roasted potatoes, steamed vegetables, or a fresh green salad.

Enjoy your flavorful and elegant Irish Lamb Chops with Mint Jelly!

Cottage Pie with Vegetables

Ingredients:

For the Meat Filling:

- 1 lb (450g) ground beef
- 1 tablespoon olive oil

- 1 large onion, chopped
- 2 cloves garlic, minced
- 2 carrots, peeled and diced
- 1 cup frozen peas
- 1 cup corn kernels (fresh or frozen)
- 1/2 cup mushrooms, diced (optional)
- 2 tablespoons tomato paste
- 1 tablespoon Worcestershire sauce
- 1 teaspoon dried thyme
- 1 teaspoon dried rosemary
- 1 cup beef broth
- Salt and black pepper to taste

For the Mashed Potatoes:

- 2 lbs (900g) potatoes (e.g., Russet or Yukon Gold), peeled and cubed
- 4 tablespoons unsalted butter
- 1/2 cup milk
- Salt and black pepper to taste

Instructions:

1. **Prepare the Mashed Potatoes:**
   - Place the peeled and cubed potatoes in a large pot and cover with cold water. Add a pinch of salt.
   - Bring to a boil over high heat. Reduce the heat and simmer until the potatoes are tender, about 15-20 minutes.
   - Drain the potatoes and return them to the pot. Mash with a potato masher until smooth.
   - Stir in the butter and milk until fully incorporated. Season with salt and black pepper to taste. Set aside.
2. **Prepare the Meat Filling:**
   - Heat olive oil in a large skillet over medium heat.
   - Add the chopped onion and cook until softened, about 5 minutes.
   - Stir in the minced garlic and cook for an additional minute.
   - Add the ground beef and cook until browned, breaking it up with a spoon as it cooks.
   - Stir in the tomato paste, Worcestershire sauce, thyme, and rosemary. Cook for 1-2 minutes.
   - Add the diced carrots, peas, corn, and mushrooms (if using). Stir to combine.
   - Pour in the beef broth and bring the mixture to a simmer. Cook for 10-15 minutes, or until the vegetables are tender and the sauce has thickened. Season with salt and black pepper to taste.
3. **Assemble the Cottage Pie:**
   - Preheat your oven to 375°F (190°C).

- Transfer the meat filling to a baking dish, spreading it out evenly.
- Spoon the mashed potatoes over the meat filling, spreading them out with a spatula. You can use a fork to create a pattern on the top if desired.
4. **Bake:**
    - Place the baking dish in the preheated oven and bake for 25-30 minutes, or until the top is golden brown and the filling is bubbling.
5. **Serve:**
    - Let the Cottage Pie cool for a few minutes before serving. This allows the filling to set and makes it easier to serve.

Tips:

- **Vegetable Variations:** Feel free to add other vegetables like green beans, parsnips, or sweet potatoes to the filling.
- **Mashed Potatoes:** For extra creaminess, you can add a bit more butter or milk to the mashed potatoes. Some people also like to stir in grated cheese.
- **Make Ahead:** You can prepare the Cottage Pie a day in advance and store it in the refrigerator. Reheat in the oven before serving.

Enjoy your comforting and hearty Cottage Pie with Vegetables!

Irish Cheddar and Chive Biscuits

Ingredients:

- 2 cups all-purpose flour
- 1 tablespoon baking powder
- 1/2 teaspoon baking soda
- 1/2 teaspoon salt

- 1/2 teaspoon black pepper
- 1/2 cup unsalted butter, cold and cut into small cubes
- 1 cup shredded Irish Cheddar cheese (or sharp cheddar)
- 1/4 cup chopped fresh chives (or 2 tablespoons dried chives)
- 3/4 cup buttermilk (or milk with 1 tablespoon lemon juice or vinegar)

Instructions:

1. **Preheat the Oven:**
   - Preheat your oven to 425°F (220°C). Line a baking sheet with parchment paper or a silicone baking mat.
2. **Prepare the Dry Ingredients:**
   - In a large mixing bowl, whisk together the flour, baking powder, baking soda, salt, and black pepper.
3. **Cut in the Butter:**
   - Add the cold, cubed butter to the flour mixture. Using a pastry cutter or your fingers, cut the butter into the flour until the mixture resembles coarse crumbs with pea-sized pieces of butter.
4. **Add Cheese and Chives:**
   - Stir in the shredded cheddar cheese and chopped chives until evenly distributed.
5. **Add the Buttermilk:**
   - Pour in the buttermilk and gently stir until the dough just comes together. Be careful not to overmix; the dough should be slightly sticky but manageable.
6. **Form the Biscuits:**
   - Turn the dough out onto a floured surface. Gently knead the dough a few times to bring it together. Pat it out to about 1-inch thickness.
   - Use a round biscuit cutter or a glass to cut out biscuits. Place them on the prepared baking sheet, close together but not touching.
7. **Bake:**
   - Bake in the preheated oven for 12-15 minutes, or until the biscuits are golden brown on top and cooked through.
8. **Cool and Serve:**
   - Remove the biscuits from the oven and let them cool slightly on a wire rack before serving.

Tips:

- **Butter:** Make sure the butter is very cold to create flaky layers in the biscuits. You can even chill the butter and flour mixture before combining.
- **Buttermilk Substitute:** If you don't have buttermilk, you can use regular milk with a tablespoon of lemon juice or vinegar. Let it sit for 5 minutes before using.
- **Cheese Variations:** Feel free to experiment with different types of cheese or add extra herbs for varied flavors.

Enjoy your flavorful and cheesy Irish Cheddar and Chive Biscuits!

Irish Baked Potatoes with Sour Cream

Ingredients:

- 4 large russet potatoes
- Olive oil
- Salt and black pepper
- 1 cup sour cream
- 2 tablespoons fresh chives, finely chopped (or 1 tablespoon dried chives)

- 1/2 cup shredded Irish Cheddar cheese (optional)
- 4 tablespoons unsalted butter (optional)
- Additional toppings (optional): crispy bacon bits, green onions, or fresh herbs

Instructions:

1. **Preheat the Oven:**
    - Preheat your oven to 425°F (220°C).
2. **Prepare the Potatoes:**
    - Scrub the potatoes thoroughly under cold water to remove any dirt. Pat them dry with a paper towel.
    - Prick each potato a few times with a fork to allow steam to escape during baking.
    - Rub the potatoes with olive oil and season generously with salt and black pepper.
3. **Bake the Potatoes:**
    - Place the potatoes directly on the oven rack or on a baking sheet lined with parchment paper.
    - Bake for 45-60 minutes, or until the potatoes are tender when pierced with a fork and the skins are crispy. The baking time may vary depending on the size of the potatoes.
4. **Prepare the Topping:**
    - While the potatoes are baking, mix the sour cream with the chopped chives in a small bowl. Season with salt and pepper to taste.
5. **Serve:**
    - Once the potatoes are done baking, remove them from the oven and let them cool slightly.
    - Cut a slit down the center of each potato and gently squeeze the sides to open them up.
    - If using, place a pat of butter on each potato and let it melt.
    - Spoon a generous amount of the sour cream mixture over each potato.
6. **Optional Toppings:**
    - Sprinkle with shredded cheddar cheese, crispy bacon bits, additional chives, or green onions if desired.

Tips:

- **Potato Size:** Choose potatoes of similar size for even cooking. If you have very large potatoes, they may need additional baking time.
- **Cheese:** For extra flavor, you can melt some cheddar cheese on the potatoes during the last 5 minutes of baking by placing the cheese on top of the potatoes before they finish baking.
- **Butter:** Adding butter enhances the flavor and richness, but it's optional depending on your preference.

Enjoy your delicious Irish Baked Potatoes with Sour Cream, perfect as a side dish or a satisfying meal on their own!

Guinness Beef Stroganoff

Ingredients:

- 1 lb (450g) beef sirloin or tenderloin, cut into thin strips
- 2 tablespoons olive oil
- 1 large onion, finely chopped
- 3 cloves garlic, minced
- 1 cup mushrooms, sliced
- 1 cup beef broth
- 1 cup Guinness stout (or another dark beer)

- 2 tablespoons all-purpose flour
- 1 tablespoon Dijon mustard
- 1 tablespoon Worcestershire sauce
- 1 teaspoon dried thyme
- 1 teaspoon paprika
- 1/2 cup sour cream
- Salt and black pepper to taste
- Fresh parsley, chopped (for garnish)
- Cooked egg noodles or rice (for serving)

Instructions:

1. **Prepare the Beef:**
   - Season the beef strips with salt and black pepper.
   - Heat olive oil in a large skillet or Dutch oven over medium-high heat.
   - Add the beef in batches (if necessary) and cook until browned on all sides. Remove the beef from the skillet and set aside.
2. **Cook the Vegetables:**
   - In the same skillet, add the chopped onion and cook until softened, about 5 minutes.
   - Stir in the minced garlic and cook for an additional minute.
   - Add the sliced mushrooms and cook until they release their moisture and become golden brown, about 5 minutes.
3. **Make the Sauce:**
   - Sprinkle the flour over the vegetables and stir to combine. Cook for 1-2 minutes to eliminate the raw flour taste.
   - Gradually pour in the Guinness stout, stirring constantly to avoid lumps.
   - Add the beef broth, Dijon mustard, Worcestershire sauce, thyme, and paprika. Stir well to combine.
   - Bring the mixture to a simmer and cook for 10-15 minutes, or until the sauce has thickened.
4. **Combine and Finish:**
   - Return the browned beef strips to the skillet and stir to coat with the sauce.
   - Reduce the heat to low and stir in the sour cream. Cook for an additional 2-3 minutes, or until the beef is heated through and the sauce is creamy. Adjust seasoning with salt and black pepper to taste.
5. **Serve:**
   - Serve the Guinness Beef Stroganoff over cooked egg noodles, rice, or mashed potatoes.
   - Garnish with chopped fresh parsley.

Tips:

- **Beef:** Use a tender cut of beef such as sirloin or tenderloin for the best results. If you use a less tender cut, consider simmering the beef longer to tenderize it.

- **Beer:** If you prefer a milder flavor, you can substitute Guinness with a lighter beer or non-alcoholic beer. The richness of Guinness adds a deep flavor, but you can adjust according to taste.
- **Sour Cream:** For a tangier flavor, you can use Greek yogurt instead of sour cream.

Enjoy your hearty and flavorful Guinness Beef Stroganoff!

Traditional Irish Roast Pork

Ingredients:

- 4-5 lb (1.8-2.3 kg) pork loin or pork shoulder with skin on
- 2 tablespoons olive oil
- 1 tablespoon sea salt (for the skin)
- 1 teaspoon black pepper
- 1 tablespoon fresh rosemary, finely chopped (or 1 teaspoon dried rosemary)
- 1 tablespoon fresh thyme, finely chopped (or 1 teaspoon dried thyme)
- 3 cloves garlic, minced
- 1 large onion, roughly chopped

- 2 carrots, peeled and cut into chunks
- 2 celery stalks, cut into chunks
- 1 cup chicken or vegetable broth
- 1 cup dry white wine or cider (optional)

Instructions:

1. **Preheat the Oven:**
    - Preheat your oven to 450°F (230°C).
2. **Prepare the Pork:**
    - Pat the pork roast dry with paper towels. This helps the skin become crispy.
    - Using a sharp knife, score the skin in a crosshatch pattern. Be careful not to cut into the meat.
    - Rub the pork skin with olive oil and season generously with sea salt, black pepper, rosemary, thyme, and minced garlic, making sure to get some seasoning into the scored cuts.
3. **Prepare the Vegetables:**
    - Place the chopped onion, carrots, and celery in the bottom of a roasting pan. These vegetables will act as a bed for the pork and add flavor to the drippings.
4. **Roast the Pork:**
    - Place the pork on top of the vegetables in the roasting pan.
    - Roast in the preheated oven for 20-30 minutes, or until the skin is crispy and golden brown. This high temperature helps to achieve the crackling.
    - After the initial high-temperature roasting, reduce the oven temperature to 350°F (175°C) and continue roasting for an additional 1-1.5 hours, or until the pork is cooked through and tender. The internal temperature should reach 145°F (63°C) for medium-rare or 160°F (71°C) for medium.
5. **Rest the Pork:**
    - Remove the pork from the oven and let it rest for at least 15 minutes before carving. This allows the juices to redistribute throughout the meat.
6. **Make the Gravy:**
    - While the pork is resting, make the gravy. Skim off any excess fat from the roasting pan, leaving about 2 tablespoons.
    - Place the pan on the stovetop over medium heat. Add a splash of white wine or cider to deglaze the pan, scraping up any browned bits from the bottom.
    - Add the chicken or vegetable broth and bring to a simmer. Reduce the liquid by half to concentrate the flavors. Optionally, you can thicken the gravy with a slurry of cornstarch and water.
7. **Serve:**
    - Carve the pork into slices and serve with the roasted vegetables and gravy.

Tips:

- **Scoring the Skin:** Make sure to score the skin deeply but not too deeply to ensure it crisps up properly. The salt rub helps to draw out moisture, aiding in the crispiness.

- **Resting Time:** Don't skip the resting time; it's crucial for juicy meat.
- **Vegetables:** The vegetables can be served alongside the pork or used to make a flavorful gravy.

Enjoy your Traditional Irish Roast Pork with its crispy crackling and tender, juicy meat!

Irish Green Beans with Bacon

Ingredients:

- 1 lb (450g) fresh green beans, trimmed and cut into bite-sized pieces
- 4 strips of bacon, diced
- 1 small onion, finely chopped
- 2 cloves garlic, minced
- 1/4 cup chicken or vegetable broth
- 1 tablespoon olive oil
- Salt and black pepper to taste
- 1 tablespoon fresh parsley, chopped (for garnish, optional)

- 1 tablespoon toasted slivered almonds or crispy fried onions (optional, for added crunch)

Instructions:

1. **Cook the Bacon:**
   - In a large skillet, cook the diced bacon over medium heat until it is crisp and browned. This should take about 5-7 minutes.
   - Remove the bacon from the skillet and drain on paper towels. Leave about 1 tablespoon of bacon drippings in the skillet.
2. **Sauté the Vegetables:**
   - In the same skillet with the bacon drippings, add the olive oil if necessary. Heat over medium heat.
   - Add the chopped onion and cook until softened and translucent, about 4-5 minutes.
   - Stir in the minced garlic and cook for an additional 1 minute.
3. **Cook the Green Beans:**
   - Add the trimmed and cut green beans to the skillet. Stir to coat with the onion and garlic mixture.
   - Pour in the chicken or vegetable broth and cover the skillet. Cook for about 5-7 minutes, or until the green beans are tender-crisp. Stir occasionally to ensure even cooking.
4. **Combine and Finish:**
   - Once the green beans are cooked to your liking, stir in the cooked bacon.
   - Season with salt and black pepper to taste. Adjust seasoning as needed.
5. **Serve:**
   - Transfer the green beans and bacon to a serving dish.
   - Garnish with chopped fresh parsley and toasted slivered almonds or crispy fried onions, if desired.

Tips:

- **Green Beans:** For extra crispness, you can blanch the green beans in boiling water for 2-3 minutes before adding them to the skillet. This helps to keep their vibrant color and texture.
- **Bacon:** For a smoky flavor, consider using smoked bacon or adding a touch of smoked paprika to the dish.
- **Crunch:** The toasted almonds or crispy fried onions add a nice crunch and additional flavor, but they are optional.

Enjoy your flavorful Irish Green Beans with Bacon, a perfect side dish that complements a variety of main courses!

Spiced Irish Lamb Stew

Ingredients:

- 2 lbs (900g) lamb shoulder or leg, trimmed and cut into 1-inch cubes
- 2 tablespoons olive oil
- 1 large onion, chopped
- 3 cloves garlic, minced
- 2 carrots, peeled and sliced
- 2 celery stalks, chopped
- 1 cup parsnips, peeled and sliced (optional)
- 1 cup turnips, peeled and cubed (optional)
- 1 tablespoon tomato paste
- 1 tablespoon all-purpose flour

- 1 teaspoon ground cumin
- 1 teaspoon ground coriander
- 1 teaspoon smoked paprika
- 1/2 teaspoon ground cinnamon
- 1/2 teaspoon ground turmeric
- 1/4 teaspoon ground cayenne pepper (optional, for heat)
- 4 cups beef or lamb broth
- 1 cup dry white wine or stout beer (optional)
- 2 bay leaves
- 1 cup frozen peas
- Salt and black pepper to taste
- Fresh parsley or thyme, chopped (for garnish)

Instructions:

1. **Prepare the Lamb:**
   - Season the lamb cubes with salt and black pepper.
   - Heat olive oil in a large Dutch oven or heavy-bottomed pot over medium-high heat.
   - Add the lamb in batches and brown on all sides. Remove the lamb and set aside.
2. **Cook the Vegetables:**
   - In the same pot, add the chopped onion and cook until softened, about 5 minutes.
   - Stir in the minced garlic and cook for another minute.
   - Add the sliced carrots, chopped celery, and optional parsnips and turnips. Cook for 5-7 minutes, stirring occasionally.
3. **Add Spices and Flour:**
   - Stir in the tomato paste and cook for 1-2 minutes.
   - Sprinkle the flour over the vegetables and spices, stirring to combine. Cook for another minute to eliminate the raw flour taste.
   - Add the cumin, coriander, smoked paprika, cinnamon, turmeric, and optional cayenne pepper. Stir well to coat the vegetables.
4. **Deglaze and Simmer:**
   - Pour in the beef or lamb broth and white wine or stout, if using. Scrape up any browned bits from the bottom of the pot.
   - Return the browned lamb to the pot and add the bay leaves.
   - Bring the stew to a simmer, then cover and cook for about 1.5 to 2 hours, or until the lamb is tender and the vegetables are cooked through.
5. **Finish the Stew:**
   - Stir in the frozen peas and cook for an additional 5 minutes.
   - Adjust seasoning with salt and black pepper to taste.
6. **Serve:**
   - Garnish with chopped fresh parsley or thyme.
   - Serve the stew with crusty bread, mashed potatoes, or over cooked rice.

Tips:

- **Lamb:** Using lamb shoulder or leg provides a good amount of flavor and tenderness. You can also use lamb stew meat from the butcher.
- **Thickening:** If you prefer a thicker stew, you can mix a tablespoon of flour or cornstarch with a small amount of water and stir it into the stew in the last 15 minutes of cooking.
- **Vegetables:** Feel free to add or substitute other root vegetables according to your preference.

Enjoy your Spiced Irish Lamb Stew, a flavorful and comforting dish perfect for any occasion!

www.ingramcontent.com/pod-product-compliance
Lightning Source LLC
LaVergne TN
LVHW081603060526
838201LV00054B/2049